SAVOUR OF IRELAND

A photographic and gastronomic tour of Ireland a century ago

GEORGE MORRISON

Period photographs and recipes specially prepared by the Author

LINDSAY PUBLICATIONS

First published 1996 by Lindsay Publications, Glasgow

ISBN 1 898169 09 8

©1996 George Morrison

With sincerest gratitude to S.F. who has restored the sight to my right eye

The moral right of the author has been asserted

All rights reserved

No part of this publication may be reproduced, stored in a retrieval system, or transmitted in any form, or by any means, electronic, mechanical, photocopying, recording or otherwise, without the express written permission of the publisher.

British Library Cataloguing-in-Publication Data
A Catalogue record for this book is available from the British Library

Designed by Mitchell Graphics, Glasgow

Printed and bound in Great Britain by Cromwell Press Limited

ACKNOWLEDGMENTS

The amount of useful information that can be obtained from a photograph is pimarily determined by the fineness of detail in the image which is mainly cirumscribed by the fineness of the grain of a given photographic process or individual emulsion. The grain structure represents the noise level and the finer it is the more favourable is the signal to noise ratio, other things being equal. Sadly, other things in this sublunary sphere almost never are equal, so that factors such as *netteté* of focus, depth of field, scatter in the emulsion and in its support and distortions in what ideally should be the straight line graph relating exposure to density all disturb the extraction of reliable information. We are indeed fortunate that, with the introduction of Scott-Archer's Wet Collodion process in 1851, a photographic emulsion that was virtually grainless was made available for the recording of visual information. The definition of the then available lenses was the next limiting factor. The application of photography to Brewster's stereoscope rapidly created a demand for photographs having a large depth of field and high definition and resulted in the appearance of a form of photography which has many inherent advantages when the extraction of information, other than that envisaged by the original photographer, is in play.

It takes a wise individual indeed to know what questions the future will seek answers for in the photographs of the present.

For some twenty years from the early 1860s the Irish Stereoscopic Company took some thousands of photographs all over Ireland and although the emulsions which were used for these are very far removed in their characteristics from those of modern emulsions and papers.

Although scatter fom the glass support and differences of refractive index still present certain problems the virtually pin-hole apertures used resulted in large depth of field and high definition negatives.

The great kindness of the late Dr Richard Hayes, Director of the National Library of Ireland, in granting me unrestricted access to these original negatives has given me the opportunity to make an exhaustive study of the optimal techniques for obtaining useful information about the past from these visual sources and has enabled me to contribute this information to a number of books and periodicals, as well as furnishing illustrative material for books of my own authorship.

I would like to record here my most grateful thanks for all his help and encouragement.

INTRODUCTION

Travelling is one of the most stimulating and refreshing activities that we know. The first hand impression of new places that it gives has a tonic effect on both mind and body that has no substitute and with which even television cannot compete. A wise man once said 'If you want to prolong your life, travel a lot, for the first week in any new place seems like a fortnight.' But the traveller who travels really sagaciously travels in time as well as in space. However fascinating a visit to any place may be, the interest is greatly enhanced by a knowledge of that place in former times. Such knowledge gives depth to our appreciation of the present and immersing ourselves, from time to time, in the past is a form of travel that even those tied to a single locality can enjoy.

Until only a hundred and sixty-five years ago, we depended entirely on the images left to us by draughtsmen, painters and sculptors for our imagery of the past and upon the verbal descriptions to be found in literature. In 1826 a new and vitally different kind of window was opened, when Nicéphore Niepce took the first permanent photograph. Through photography it became possible, mechanically, to record visual information directly, without its having to pass through the conditioned visual hypotheses of a graphic artist and so we could gain a more direct and unprejudiced perception of the appearance of former times, as well as freeing ourselves from certain blinkers that restricted our visual awareness for millennia; such as how a horse gallops. The 'picturesqueness' of ragged people assumes quite a different character in a photograph from that portrayed by a graphic artist. One can almost smell rags in a photograph. That very 'mechanical' character of much early photography, which was harshly criticized by many painters of the period, turns out to be a sterling quality that greatly aids us in getting a truer, fuller view of the real appearance of things in times gone by. Likewise the ways in which the more opulent classes dressed and behaved are often better conveyed in photographs than in drawings. This book is intended to open the photographic window on the past a little wider.

Scott-Archer's 'wet-collodion' process of 1851, a modified form of which was used by many photographers of the ensuing period, has a special quality which makes it particularly useful for social research; it is virtually grainless and so has a very favourable signal to noise ratio. This quality, together with the fact that stereoscopic photographs of the period demanded maximum depth of field and a high resolution image which could only be achieved, with the lenses of the time, by the use of a nearly pin-hole aperture, enable us, today, to make very big enlargements of small areas of the original photographs and so search out information that would be denied to us by graininess or soft focus. To get the best results, one must prepare the master duplicates by means of a special technique, as the characteristic density curves of the period negatives are quite different from those of most present day photographic materials. To maximize the extracting of information, a special regime derived from a densitometric scan of each negative must be the starting point for the making of the photo-restoration masters from which the ultimate prints or transparencies are produced. This is a skilled, painstaking and labour intensive process, but one that avoids some of the losses entailed in computer enhancement as well as the danger, inherent in the latter technique, of 'painting' or modifying the image in a subjective manner. Computer image-enhancement has many advantages where quick results are needed, but is best performed, on old material, by an operator with a good knowledge of the period who can avoid misinterpretation of detail and the introduction of artifacts.

Prepared in this way, the original materials afford an astonishing richness of detail which can give us surprising insights into the real life of times long gone in the fields of topography, agriculture, afforestation and transportation but, above all, we see the appearance, costume and manners of living people, at once so like and yet so tremendously different from ourselves. It is this difference, increasing directly with the passage of time, that is the secret of the real fascination that we experience in viewing the details of old photographs, not their 'nostalgic' appeal, which is a shallow emotion extending only to a lifetime. The real strangeness of the past is the key which unlocks our curiosity and enthralment.

Much of the attraction of Ireland is the direct result of its insular situation. All but the very earliest inhabitants were obliged to reach it by crossing the sea and sea-faring peoples played a very prominent part in establishing the unique cultural mix that we associate with the country today. The megalithic peoples who voyaged around and settled on so many parts of the Atlantic seaboard of Europe brought us our first artists. They left us, in Slieve na Calliagh and Newgrange, one of the most glorious bodies of megalithic art to be found anywhere. The Bronze and Iron Age settlers brought further enrichment before the early Christians contributed their Coptic and Greek-influenced art, which was to exercise such a powerful effect on that of the Vikings, which would, in its turn, revivify Irish art at the time when it was to attain the apogee of its splendour, just before and during the appearance of the Romanesque. The Romans, themselves, did not occupy Ireland, so their influence was only an indirect one, a factor which is also one of the reasons for the particular flavour of the Irish scene which present day travellers find so individual, as did the travellers in the last century.

The year 1860 has been chosen as a beginning because it was in that year that a regular scheduled train service of eleven hours, London Euston to the Carlisle Pier, Kingstown (now and formerly Dunlaoghaire) was established. Our prospective visitors would have passed beneath the great pylon at Euston to take what was to become the longest running named-train in the history of railways, the 'Irish Mail'. It began its service on the first of August 1848, leaving Euston at 8.45 p.m., a departure time that remained unchanged until August 1939. Corridor trains had not yet been introduced but passengers, having ascertained that the foot-warmers in their compartment had been filled, would have arranged for a basket containing a packed cold collation to be provided before the train left. Unknown to most of those travelling, a very important registered-postal-packet was put aboard each evening just before departure. It was a sealed chronometer, set every day at Greenwich Observatory on the zero Meridian to Greenwich Mean Time, from which the master clock in the G.P.O. Dublin was kept at that time. All the Irish railways used this clock for their scheduling as distinct from the local Dunsink time in general use. Our visitors would have arrived at the port of Holyhead at 2.35 a.m., where they would transfer to what were then the first steamers anywhere in the world to exceed 18 knots and which left for Ireland at or before 3.00 a.m. to arrive at 6.45 a.m. Let us take up the story as one of them enters Kingstown Harbour.

P.S. Connaught entering Kingstown Harbour at 6.25 a.m. on a summer morning in the early 1860s.

THIS SHIP WAS THE FASTEST STEAMER IN THE WORLD AT THIS TIME and, the weather being calm, could make the crossing of the Irish Sea, from Holyhead, in less than three and a quarter hours, a better time than that made by the roll on-roll off ferries of today! It looks as though the passengers have had a smooth crossing, so some of them may already have had breakfast. A breakfast dish offered on board these vessels being Finnian Haddie poached in milk with a poached egg mounted on top, a tradition continued on the London Midland and Scottish Railway turbine steamers that operated the service in the 1920s and 1930s. Everyone will be gathering up their luggage as the vessel will be alongside the Carlisle Pier in not more than four minutes. The service was run by the City of Dublin Steam Packet Company who held the Royal Mail contract from 1850 until 1920 and who maintained a regular scheduled service in all weathers. Even in the most severe conditions their paddle-steamers were never more than a few minutes late in arriving. Two of the *Connaught*'s sister ships, the *Ulster* and the *Munster*, were, like herself, built in Birkenhead. The remaining vessel, the *Leinster*, was London built. These Royal Mail paddle steamers were much more popular than the slower paddle steamers operated by the London & North Western Railway Company, as the City of Dublin Steam Packet Company's vessels were not only faster but much better appointed, with First Class Saloons 60 feet in length and luxuriously upholstered. They were built with turtle foredecks to throw off the water in heavy weather and were so successful on this service, which can be very rough in the winter, that they were re-boilered and converted to twin-funnel ships in the 1880s, continuing in service until the Company replaced them with twin-screw steamers bearing the same names in the 1890s. Their paddle-boxes helped to stabilize them in roll, a feature which made some travellers prefer them to their successors, though these, too, were the fastest passenger steamers in the world in their day and could make the crossing in two and three-quarter hours in most weather. Specially scheduled mail trains were run by the Irish railway companies and a large force of porters stood by at the Carlisle Pier to transfer the mails as rapidly as possible to the trains, and so rapidly could this be done that the passengers had only just comfortable time to take their seats before the trains left. As the vessel arrives, those on deck will have seen the Royal Navy guard ship of the harbour which the paddle-steamer has just passed.

H.M.S. Royal George *on harbour guard duty, Kingstown (now Dunlaoghaire) Harbour*

At first glance this 'wooden walls' man of war, with its two decks of muzzle-loading cannon, seems to resemble a warship of the time of the Battle of Trafalgar, nearly fifty years previously. It had been named in succession to Admiral Kempenfeldt's unlucky flagship, which went down while being careened at Portsmouth with very heavy loss of life, many sailors' wives being among the drowned. A closer look reveals interesting features. In the men-o-war of the eighteenth century, space below, between decks, was very crowded and cramped, which alone was a cause of much ill health and serious disease among the sailors who worked the ships, often under severe conditions of storm or tropical heat. The two great alleviations of their condition were the introduction of lime-juice as an antiscorbutic and the improvement of below-decks ventilation, which helped to reduce the high incidence of many lung diseases.

To increase ventilation for the men below decks on vessels of the eighteenth century and during the Napoleonic Wars, it was common practice to fit a 'wind sail' or spread of canvas set at an angle over a hatchway to deflect a current of air down the hatch and promote the circulation of air on the lower decks. With the coming of steam, the fires of the boiler furnaces made large demands upon the air supply of the stokeholds to maintain a sufficient supply of oxygen to keep the fires burning at maximum heat. An air demand far greater than that required by crews. This led to the rapid development of the cowled ventilator, at first found only on steamers, but later fitted to sailing vessels and particularly those carrying auxilliary steam engines.

The old method of increasing ventilation, the 'wind-sail' is seen mounted just abaft the fore-mast, while the four large metal cowl ventilators strongly suggest that the *Royal George* had been fitted with boilers and an auxiliary steam engine and screw. The apparent absence of a funnel does not contradict this view as, at this time, sailing vessels with an auxilliary engine often carried a de-mountable funnel which was only seen when their boilers were in use.

Though warships of this kind had long ceased to be fast and manoeuvrable enough to keep up with the mid-nineteenth century fleet, they were still serviceable as easily moveable harbour protection vessels, stationed, with their considerable fire-power of short-range muzzle-loading cannon, in the major ports around the British Isles. Many remained at this task well into the 1880s, while some were converted into prison transports.

The ships carrying those sentenced to transportation to the antipodal prison colonies used to lie at anchor close to the guard ship, waiting to take on their unhappy freight. Thackeray, in his *Irish Sketchbook* of 1844, mentions seeing a crowd of prisoners lining the rail of the transport in Kingstown Harbour to watch a regatta taking place.

R.M.P.S. Connaught *alongside the Carlisle Pier*

THE CARLISLE PIER WAS SPECIALLY BUILT IN 1959 TO FACILITATE the transfer of the mails and passengers between the railway and the mail boats. A little later a spur from the railway was built down onto the pier itself and passengers had only to cross the platform to have immediate access to the steamers, a convenience particularly appreciated by those encumbered with luggage. Coras Iompar Eireann removed this spur a few years ago thus obliging foot-passengers to make a considerable walk from Dunlaoghaire station, after which they are forced to walk down and up stairways in the new ferry terminal, a very considerable inconvenience which represents a serious falling off in service.

As soon as the mail-boats made fast, three gangways were run aboard, one for passengers to disembark and the other two for the transference of the mails from the ship to the trains with the greatest possible speed. A continuous procession of porters boarded the ship by one gangway, carrying with them the mails from Ireland. They returned ashore laden with the arriving mails destined for the trains and this continued until, in a very few minutes, both lots of mails had been transferred and the ship and the trains set out upon their return journeys.

From 1860 until the outbreak of the First World War, between it and the Second World War and even for some years after the latter, a letter posted anywhere in Dublin before 6.00 p.m. and even later if posted in a late-fee box, would be delivered to any address in London at breakfast time the following day and vice-versa. A letter posted in any town in Ireland before noon would be delivered to any town in England before noon on the following day and this, with the exception of the late-fee boxes, at the very moderate normal postal charges. It is no compensation for the serious deterioration in service at the present time to tell us that we are enjoying a better service when common sense clearly tells us that we are not. The lack of this most cost-effective system of original document transfer is not made up for by the fax service, as those who have no access to fax machines at both ends are effectively disenfranchised and have to have recourse to private courier services, as they did in the eighteenth century, at a correspondingly exorbitant cost. This amounts to an involutionary change, increasing income-based class distinctions in telecommunications. The 'penny post' was a great democratic social concept which worked well. The erosion of this system, without the substitution of one having an equal degree of cheap public access from the nearest post-box, is a serious matter with profound social consequences. There is no technical reason to move backwards. What is needed is for public ownership to improve its communications services as it did in the past with the 'penny post' and bring that great institution fully into the electronic age.

Conversation on the way to the train, Salthill and Monkstown station, Dublin. C. 1865

This line was the first railway to be built and operated in Ireland, opening its service to the public on 17 December 1834. It remained an independent company for over ninety years, the third longest lasting railway company in the British Isles, only being merged with the Great Southern Railway in 1925. In the 1870s, when this photograph was taken, traffic on it was worked, under a leasing agreement, by the Dublin, Wicklow and Wexford Railway. The figures in the foreground, one of whom is a young nurse-maid with an interesting tricycle pram, are not standing on the station platform but on an extensive esplanade that ran along the coast and to which access was gained by foot-bridges across the railway. The embankment and sea-wall were needed for the greater part of this line and were constructed by the original company, making it a very expensive railway to build but so well was the work done that its costs were fully recovered over the many years of the company's long ownership. The advertisement refers to concerts that were held during the summer on the East Pier at Kingstown Harbour, tickets for which, including the return train fare, could be bought at the ticket-offices at the stations.

The large building on the high ground is the Salthill Hotel, then run by a Mr Lovegrove, where William Makepeace Thackeray spent a night with friends, enjoying a dinner, the chief dish of which was lobster cooked in butter and sherry in a 'dispatcher' or closed chafing-dish heated by a spirit lamp. He was at the start of his tour of Ireland for his *Irish Sketchbook* of 1844, in which he gives the recipe, which begins:

'You take a lobster, about three feet long if possible, remove the shell, cut or break the flesh of the fish in pieces not too small. Some one else meanwhile makes a mixture of mustard, vinegar, catsup and lots of cayenne pepper . . .' *O tempora - O mores!* What a way to treat such a fine and delicate shellfish! Not surprisingly he adds the postscript 'N.B. You are recommended not to hurry yourself in getting up, next morning, and may take soda-water with advantage. *Probatum est!*' So I should imagine.

The whole of this southern stretch of Dublin Bay had restaurants specializing in fish dishes and although the Salthill Hotel was burned down in 1973, present day travellers may enjoy far more civilized and excellent lobster dishes in the Restaurant na Mara at the railway station in Dunlaoghaire or the Guinea Pig in Dalkey. The railway, which provided our imagined travellers convenient access to Dublin, still offers it today, on a more frequent schedule than it did in Thackeray's time.

Sackville St (O'Connell St) Dublin, 1856

Francis Johnson's powerful, dignified and yet graceful building to replace Dublin's original General Post Office was commenced in 1814 and opened for public business in 1818. It was here that the master clock kept at Greenwich Mean Time, checked against the daily delivered chronometers (v. page 5) was housed, in the main central hall. Here too terminated the electric-telegraph, laid by submarine cable to Holyhead in 1852 and thence connected to London. This splendid building, having been made the Republican headquarters in the Easter Rising of 1916, was almost totally destroyed by bombardment with eighteen-pounder shells. After 1922 it was carefully rebuilt, but with certain changes to the upper storey, fortunately hidden from street level by the balustrade. It was reopened for public use in 1929. To the right is the Nelson Pillar, erected as a memorial to the Admiral in 1808, from the designs of Francis Johnson and the architect Wilkins. The small square area on which it is seen standing was made the property of the Nelson family, to whom moneys deriving from the tiny admission fee accrued and were used by them to maintain the memorial. The Pillar was partly demolished in 1966 by an explosion organised by Republican activists and intended to commemorate the Easter Rising.

This photograph is also of great interest as it shows Sackville Street before the introduction of the horse trams. A horse omnibus service had been in operation from 1858. It is also one of the earliest photographs to show a Brougham plying for hire in a Dublin street. In Fox Talbot's photographs of Dublin, only two-wheeled 'inside' and 'outside' cars are seen. Both were of a very light construction so that a single animal could pull them over the rough surfaces of the streets, some of which were still unmetalled and in winter were filled with mud.

To pull the much heavier four-wheeled Brougham over rough, cobbled streets was more than could be expected of a single horse, so it was not until much street improvement had taken place that this vehicle, pulled by a single horse, began to appear in any numbers. Gas street lighting had been introduced in 1825 and one of the graceful, original lamp standards can be seen just to the right of the farthest column of the General Post Office portico. Regrettably, few of these fine standards are to be seen today. Electric lighting did not appear in Dublin until 1882, when the first electric arc-lamps were seen there.

A 'crossing' near the entrance to Dublin Castle, C. 1865

Dublin Castile was begun in 1204, becoming the seat of British administration in Ireland. It was frequently enlarged and this continued even after 1922. Further re-edification has taken place in recent years. Throughout its history Viceroys and General Governors of Ireland resided here, before the building of the Vice-Regal Lodge in the Phoenix Park and their courts were held in this building. Many important state prisoners were held here, including the most colourful of them all, the rebel Thomas FitzGerald, Deputy Lord Deputy, known as 'Silken Thomas'. It was the first public building to have a clock in Ireland, a clock presented by Queen Elizabeth I. The refurbished State Apartments are well worth a visit today.

A plenitude of horse-drawn traffic in a rainy climate ensures that the roadways of a town will, inevitably, be mucky even when municipal cleaning is taking place. When this situation is found at a time when the length of clothes of both men and women is close to the ground, a serious problem results. In many parts of Dublin drainage and street cleaning left much to be desired in the middle of the last century; even before the very gates of Dublin Castle. The provision of specially paved crossings, in this case composed of granite setts a little above the level of the roadway, to assist people to cross without getting their shoes and clothes filthy was an essential part of all city streets. The crossing-sweepers had the task of keeping these brushed clean. It was customary to give him or her a small tip and these casual and uncertain emoluments were their main source of livelihood. The work was undertaken mainly by children or the aged and was regarded as the most humble of the 'honest trades', the bottom of the acknowledged social scale; hence the minatory remark of the Victorian parent: 'If you do not mend your ways you will end your days as a crossing-sweeper!'

In Dublin the use of granite setts for this purpose long preceded their employment as a setting for the tram lines, which were introduced in the 1860s, a pair of horses pulling a single, four-wheeled car. The setts used for the latter purpose were smaller and more cubical in form and continued in use until the cessation of tramway services in Dublin in 1948, an electrified system having replaced the horse-drawn cars from the turn of the century. The material used was fine Wicklow granite drawn from quarries in the hills to the south west of the city.

The position of the statue of Justice over the gate was the origin of the Dublin witticism 'Justice, with her face to the Viceroy and her back to the people'.

The Corner of St Stephen's Green, near the top of Grafton Street, Dublin, C. 1865

Our visiting tourists would have found three ways of getting about Dublin other than by walking. Horse-trams, Broughams and side-cars or, to give them their full title, outside cars.

The horse-trams, regular and cheap, had an enclosed car with upholstered seats. On the top of this were wooden seats open to the weather. On a sunny day no better way could be found of viewing the Dublin streets than from one of these outside seats. On cold and rainy days the relatively small enclosed car became rapidly very crowded.

An outside car is seen in the foreground. These last were not so called from the fact that the driver and passengers were fully exposed to the prevailing weather, their only protection being a leather apron across their knees, but from the fact that the passengers' legs dangled down, outside the pair of wheels, to a foot-board. The four-wheeled Brougham had only come into use in Dublin some fifteen years previously, before which the only vehicles plying for public hire that gave any protection from the weather had been the inside-cars, a form of two-wheeled trap with a light canvas or leather covered hood on a light wooden frame. In this vehicle, the passengers' legs were inside the wheels and accommodation was exceedingly cramped. The only way that passengers could see the world outside was through a small aperture in the front or by peeping through the curtains that closed the rear of the confined space. These are the vehicles, in England called 'jingles', that were accustomed to back up against the edge of the kerb to allow their passengers to descend onto the foot-path and so avoid the mire of the roadway. In doing so, the inside car, having only a single pair of wheels, had a tendency to tip down at the back so that, in the words of Charles Dickens 'They tip their passengers out onto the pavement like a load of coals!' In fine weather sight-seers preferred the outside car or side-car as it came to be known. Both the inside and outside cars, being very light, could be pulled over rough roads by a single horse. Broughams quickly replaced the cramped inside cars in Dublin, but the latter lingered on in country towns as we shall see (page 53). The Dublin slang term for the Brougham cab was 'a growler', so called because of the reverberant noise heard inside as the originally steel-tyred wheels ran over the cobble-stones and the granite setts of the crossings and tram-lines. As the weather is fine, we can imagine that our travelling family will take a side-car for the day to see some of the sights around Dublin.

Sorrento Terrace and the Dublin Wicklow and Wexford Railway, C. 1865

To visit the well known beauty spots and antiquities of County Wicklow, in the days before the car and the motor-coach, our visitors would take the train southwards, from Dublin, past the port where they had arrived. After passing Dalkey, the line gives superb views along the coast, of which this is the first that they would see after emerging from the tunnel under Dalkey Hill.

The railway was first extended from Kingstown to Dalkey at the southern tip of Dublin Bay and then down along the coast to Bray. The great railway engineer, Isambard Kingdom Brunel, became interested in promoting a line running from Wexford, at the south-easternmost tip of Ireland, up to Dublin, to increase the traffic on his Great Western Railway. Although he did not live to see it completed, such a line was built by what eventually became the Dublin, Wicklow and Wexford Railway. Here we see it running in a cutting through Dalkey Hill.

The line between Dublin and Wexford is by far the most beautiful and picturesque railway journey that can be made in Ireland and our sagacious travellers after their visit to Dublin would have been well advised to take this route south. The agreements with the property owners along the coastal stretch required the railway company to build foot-bridges giving the owners of the land access to the beach and one of them is seen here. It is astonishing to us to see how denuded of trees this stretch of coast was a century ago. Sorrento Terrace had not yet been quite completed when this mid-1860s photograph was taken. The lack of vegetation is useful in disclosing to us the recently filled in shafts of the minor eighteenth-century lead mine which then existed under the promontory and under Dalkey Hill. The sites of these shafts have long ceased to be visible but the adit of the mine still opens onto Killiney beach close to what used to be called the Gentlemens' Bathing Place. The small white cottage, here seen in L-shaped form, was originally a miner's cottage and did not assume its two-storied structure until the 1870s. It was later, for many years, the home of the distinguished playwright and theatre director Mr Lennox Robinson. It will be seen that an iron ladder and two muzzle-loading guns are still mounted on the Martello tower on Dalkey Island, which remained garrisoned later than any of the other Irish Martello towers, it is said through the oversight of a filing clerk at the Admiralty.

The unusual use of tie-bars instead of sleepers for the railway permanent-way is very well shown in this photograph. The railway was, and still is, twin track as far as Bray, County Wicklow, after which it becomes a single track all the way to Wexford.

Guests at the Royal Hotel, Glendalough, County Wicklow, C. 1865

GLENDALOUGH, LIKE KILLARNEY AND THE GIANT'S CAUSEWAY, had been accustomed to receiving tourists from abroad since the eighteenth century. It is quite a long drive from the nearest railhead at Rathdrum, which the Dublin, Wicklow and Wexford Railway reached in 1861. This drive had, for most people, to be made by outside-car. The year round tourist market, greatly increased by the improvement in communications resulting from the expanding railway networks, brought about a big increase in the number of hotels and many of the inns surviving from the eighteenth century burgeoned into hotels. The Royal Hotel was especially favourably placed as the distance from the railhead encouraged overnight stays. The railways also brought about a change of clientèle, for a much greater number of the middle classes were able to travel to places which had hitherto been accessible only to the rich. The rigid conventions of dress which ruled in the middle of the last century did not make things any easier for those travellers. The ladies' long dresses made care necessary to avoid them catching in brambles and undergrowth and the gentlemens' silk hats needed much attention if they got wet or dirty and required a bulky hat-box to keep them safe from dinges when not being worn. Under these conditions the well appointed hotel at Glendalough was a welcome sight at the end of a long drive on an open side-car and being right next to the historical site, allowed ladies as well as their companions an easy access.

Situated in a deep hollow in the surrounding mountains, Glendalough has a microclimate all its own, with a rather higher incidence of cloud and rainfall than most of County Wicklow. This is not much of an inconvenience to the plastic-wrapped modern traveller, but in the days when women were wrapped in yards of absorbent cloth and men wore easily ruined, fragile tall hats, to have a hotel within hastening distance of such an historic site was a great reassurance. These silk hats were not only fragile, but their glossy surface could very readily be damaged and their replacement was an expensive item in a middle-class budget. Their manufacture needed the use of mercury to attain that curious glossy finish. Many hatters suffered from chronic mercury poisoning, hence the expression 'mad as a hatter!'

Some of the Staff of the Royal Hotel, Glendalough, C. 1860

As well as improvements in transport, the state visit of Queen Victoria and the Prince Consort in 1851 greatly stimulated tourism and in the years following upon their visit, the eighteenth-century inn at Glendalough was extensively rebuilt and extended and became the Royal Hotel, appearing in the 1860s very much as it does today. It is interesting to note that, in this photograph, taken not long after the rebuilding was completed, it has not yet begun to display the word 'Royal' in its title. Here, in the foreground we see a number of the staff of the hotel, including the chef, assembled. The angle of the sun tells us that the time is around 11.30 a.m. and the smoke from the kitchen chimneys, that lunch is in the course of preparation. In the interests of our travellers, let us hope that the photographer is not too fussy and will not keep the chef from the kitchen for too long!

Braised Duck

1 duck (about 2Kg.)
2 small heads of lettuce, chopped
2 tablespoons butter (or oil)
half tablespoon of freshly chopped mint
1 tablespoon of seasoned flour
half tablespoon of freshly chopped parsley
600ml. duck-giblet stock
1 egg yolk beaten with 2 tablespoons of cream
450g. freshly shelled peas
salt and freshly ground black pepper
1g. freshly grated nutmeg

(Serves 4)

Wipe the duck inside and out and joint it, then rub the pieces with the seasoned flour, heat the butter or oil and brown the duck joints all over and put them into a casserole. Put the chopped herbs into the stock and bring it to the boil, season to taste, then pour it over the duck joints. Cover the casserole and cook in the oven at 180°C. (350°F) Gas Mark 4 for about 20 minutes. Add the peas and lettuce to the casserole and cook for a further hour or so until the duck is tender. Remove casserole from oven, add the nutmeg and check again for seasoning. Make sure the casserole is not boiling and, over a very low heat, stir in the egg and cream mixture, mixing well, but on no account let the juices boil. Serve some of the sauce separately in a sauce-boat.

The guide shows the 'Deer Stone' to a visitor to Glendalough, Circa 1870

At Glendalough, County Wicklow, is found the most famous and one of the most complete remains of an early Christian monastery. It grew up as a cluster of wattle-and-mud huts surrounding the original, supposedly wooden, church near the hermitage of a sixth-century anchorite, St Kevin, said to have inhabited what authorities have described as a Mediterranean-type tomb excavated in the cliff face, on the south shore of the Upper Lake. This rock-cut tomb can still be visited today, but it is most advisable to avail of the services of a local guide, as the access is difficult and not without danger. The granite stone seen in the foreground, with an artificial, bowl-shaped circular depression, is known as a 'bullaun' and may have been used for grinding food grains or pigments or as a holy water stoup, the first being, most probably, the original function. Such stones are often found at ancient sites in Ireland from Neolithic times onwards. Tradition asserts that, at a time when the saint was without any food, a doe allowed herself to be milked into the hollow by St Kevin. In the centre background is seen the ninth century church dedicated to the saint, which has a rare surviving example of an attached, round bell tower. Beyond it, on the left, is the Glendalough Round Tower. It had lost its conical roof in the eighteenth century, but this was restored in 1874 by the Board of Works.

These towers, so characteristic of early Irish monastic sites, had their entrance doors set in the wall well out of the reach of a man standing at ground level as they were used as refuges against raiding parties in the early years of Irish monasticism. A series of wooden floors, reached by ladders, were originally built within them, the top floor serving as a belfry and point of observation.

There are some fine Romanesque doorways to be seen on the site, particularly at the cathedral.

Thomas Moore has been less than kind to this very beautiful region: 'Glendalough, whose gloomy shore skylark never warbles o'er . . .' is certainly not true today, as I have heard the bird there, though it is not, perhaps, its preferred habitat. The upper lake is particularly beautiful, cradled in a valley of the mountains and surrounded by hanging woods, but travellers of the late eighteenth and early nineteenth century and the Romantic movement affected to find wild nature terrible and grim. How tastes have changed!

A conversation at the bridge, Glenmalure, County Wicklow, C. 1865

As in the mountainous areas of the south and west, the hilly County of Wicklow had always been a centre of resistance to British rule. The great Gaelic tuath of the O'Tooles and that of the O'Byrnes had made of the remote valleys a stronghold from which descents could be launched upon the settlers of the English 'pale' or fortified enclosure. A situation which gave rise to the English expression of someone being 'beyond the pale', meaning outlandish or socially unacceptable. This state of affairs continued from Viking times right up to the eighteenth century and only came to an end on the suppression of the 1798 rising. After the rising, a long military road was built from Rathfarnham, on the outskirts of Dublin, up and through the Wicklow Mountains, continuing to the southernmost range of the hills. Looking at this photograph of a peaceful conversation between a tourist and a local farmer, it is hard to realize that less than a century earlier things were so very different. The farmer looks prosperous. He is smoking a china-clay pipe of the kind then universally used by country people of both sexes, for women smoked heavily as well as men. In rainy weather the pipe was smoked with the bowl inverted. These mountain pastures were long known for the delicious quality of the lamb reared on the hills. Wicklow lamb is still famous today.

Crusty Roast Lamb

1 shoulder of lamb (1.5-2 Kg.)
700g. potatoes, peeled and sliced
1 cup of fresh breadcrumbs
1 large onion, peeled and sliced
1 generous pinch each of very finely
 chopped rosemary and marjoram
1 large cooking apple, cored, peeled and sliced
1 good sprig of parsley, finely chopped
300 ml. lamb or chicken stock
100g. of softened butter or margarine
salt and freshly ground black pepper to taste

(Serves 6 - 8)

Wipe the lamb over and cut criss-cross slits in its upper surface. Mix together the butter, herbs, salt, pepper and breadcrumbs. Vigorously rub the mixture into the top of the joint, pressing down well so that it sticks to the scored surface. Fill the bottom of the roasting pan with the prepared vegetables and apple, mixing them and seasoning well. Put the prepared joint on top and pour the stock over the vegetables but not over the meat. Cover loosely with a sheet of kitchen foil and roast in an oven pre-heated to 200°C. (400°F)., Gas Mark 6, for half an hour. Then lower the heat to 180° C. (350°F.), Gas Mark 4 and cook for a further 20 - 25 minutes per 0.5Kg. Take the foil off for the last half hour, checking that the vegetables are nearly cooked and finish the cooking without the foil to let the outside of the roast get brown and crusty.

The Woodenbridge Hotel drag setting out for Woodenbridge Station, C. 1865

As its name implies, Woodenbridge was the hamlet which grew up around what was then an important early bridge across the Avonmore River, a few miles south of Thomas Moore's famous 'Meeting of the Waters'. In fact the junction of the Ow River with the Avonmore at Woodenbridge is known as the 'Southern Meeting of the Waters' and the old trestle-bridge provided a crossing point of the Avonmore for Wexford bound coaches.

A third river joins the Avonmore at Woodenbridge. It is known as the Gold Mines River and has a romantic association attached to it, for it was on its banks that the celebrated Irish gold rush of 1796 took place. It is now thought possible that much of the ancient Irish gold was mined in this part of County Wicklow, but those ancient sources had been long forgotten, until in the early 1790s, a school master of a remote school on the northern flank of Croghan Kinshela Mountain, called Donohue, discovered gold in the little stream running down the mountainside. He kept his discovery a dark secret and quietly exploring the bed of the stream collected an unknown quantity of nuggets which he discreetly disposed of in Dublin, but after a year or two his secret got out and in 1795 and the following year a real gold rush developed when it was found that the alluvium of the stream banks were also gold-bearing. Panning for gold started in real earnest with small concessions being sold to local people by the riparian owners and tents and temporary habitations being established on the banks of the stream. A substantial quantity of gold was obtained but exactly how much is not known on account of the lawlessness and chaos resulting from the gold rush before the government stepped in and endeavoured to regularize the situation. However one nugget of $22\frac{1}{2}$ ounces was recorded and it is assumed that even larger ones had been found earlier. The efforts of Government to regularize matters were not very successful before the 1798 rebellion broke out and operations were suspended. After the suppression of the rising a distinguished geologist was commissioned to try to find the location of a supposed quartz reef in the rock of the mountain which would have explained the source of the alluvial deposits but no such reef was ever found and it is now thought that the gold was borne to the locality with other debris by a glacier and deposited there as the ice melted.

Having completed their visit to the hilly country of Wicklow, our tourists would have had, at this time, no through rail connection to Waterford to enable them to continue their trip around Ireland, but would have had to return from Woodenbridge to Dublin to get a through rail connection.

The Tholsel, Kilkenny, County Kilkenny, C.1865

IN THE MID-EIGHTEEN-SIXTIES, OUR TRAVELLERS WOULD HAVE HAD the option of breaking their train journey to Waterford with a stop at Kilkenny, one of the earliest and historic towns in Ireland, which takes its name from the cell of St Canice, Cill Cianneach in Gaelic, around which first a monastery and later a town came into existence. Here, unlike all the large port cities of Ireland, the Vikings played a less prominent role. It was the coming of the Normans that led to the accelerated growth of the town. The original wooden motte-and-bailey Norman castle, built by Strongbow in 1172 to command a crossing-place on the River Nore, was replaced by a stone-built castle enclosing and defending the town, by his heir William le Mareschall in 1204, from whom it passed in succession to several Norman families until, in 1391, it was bought by James Butler the 3rd Earl of Ormonde. Its importance as a trade and administrative centre led to its rapid expansion beyond the castle enclosure. James I accorded Kilkenny the status of a city and its eventual commercial importance is demonstrated by the imposing Tholsel, built in 1761 to provide quarters for a Town Hall and trade exchange.

Kilkenny had been the seat of several Anglo-Irish Parliaments in mediaeval times, one in 1366, introducing the draconian 'Statutes of Kilkenny' which forbade the intermarriage of the inhabitants of the English-dominated parts of Ireland with the still Gaelic-speaking indigenous population and even contained sumptuary laws prohibiting the inhabitants of the 'Pale' from dressing like the Irish or cutting their hair in Irish style! In the English Civil War, Kilkenny declared for the King and was besieged by Cromwell, who, on its surrender treated it with much greater leniency than he showed at Drogheda.

In consequence of Cromwell's restraint, one may see in the High Street and in other parts of the city many remaining sixteenth- and seventeenth-century houses, some recently carefully restored. The Roth House and also Kyteler's Inn are excellent examples and the Civic Regalia and Muniments of the city may be seen today at the Tholsel.

The proximity to the River Nore has for long made it a place where salmon-trout and salmon are understood. Here is a local recipe for an excellent sauce for both fish.

Cucumber Sauce

1 small cucumber
2 teaspoons of fresh tarragon finely chopped
150ml double cream
salt and freshly ground white pepper

Make sure that all the ingredients are quite cold (but not frozen). Peel the cucumber (discarding the skin) and grate it into a seive to drain, with a light scattering of salt mixed in. Beat the cream until thick and then add the chopped taragon while continuing to beat, season to taste but allow for the light salting of the cucumber, which should only be mixed in just before serving with the fish.

Kilkenny from a Church Steeple, C. 1865

The steeple from which this view of Kilkenny was taken is seen at the bottom left of the photograph of High Street and the Tholsel on page 32 and the view-point shows how greatly the town has grown since the time of William le Mareschall. Looking across the roofs we can see in the distance the castle which once enclosed it. Hardly any city in Ireland has had such a varied and interesting history. It is sad to relate that to Kilkenny must fall the invidious distinction of being the town where the Inquisition and witch-burning was introduced into Ireland when a woman called Petronella of Meath was burnt at the stake there on the third of November, 1324.

The story begins some years previously and though the written sources upon which we have to rely are hardly to be described as impartial, events seem to have taken the following course. Among the powerful Norman families there would appear to have been many adherents to that surviving heathen Dianic cult so well described by the anthropologist Dr Margaret Murray in her books *The Witch Cult in Western Europe* and *The Divine King in England*. Adherents to this religion were to be found at all social levels from labouring men and women to the highest Officers of State. The most prominent figure in Kilkenny was a lady whose maiden name was Dame Alice Kyteler, belonging to an old Anglo-Norman family whose name originally appears to have been Keteller. She married first a banker by the name of Outlawe and by him had her favourite child, a son called William. She made three further marriages, the last of which was to Sir John le Poer. She undoubtedly did not show impartiality in distributing the family wealth, the bulk of which she diverted to her son William. She is said to have, with a broomstick, swept the streets of Kilkenny towards her son's door singing:

'To the house of William My sonne
Hie all the wealth of Kilkennie towne.'

This partiality appears to have been one of the circumstances leading to some of the children of her later marriages making a complaint to the then Bishop of Ossory that their fathers had been murdered by her and that her living husband, Sir John le Poer had been rendered an idiot by the administration of poison and that she was a witch. So powerful were her family that the bishop was unable to have her brought to trial and she escaped to England where she appears to have ended her life peacefully. Not so did it go with her less well-connected followers, many of whom were tortured and burnt at the stake, the first thus to die being Petronella of Meath.

The Great Picture Gallery, Kilkenny Castle, C. 1855

The Geraldines and the Butlers were the two great Irish noble families who left their mark on Irish history more than any others; often as rivals for power and influence. Kilkenny Castle was the chief Butler seat from 1391 almost until the outbreak of the Second World War. The castle was extensively rebuilt at different times but principally in the nineteenth century, when the great picture gallery was constructed to the plans of the Cork architect Benjamin Woodward. Kilkenny Castle contained one of the finest privately owned art collections in Ireland, unhappily dispersed in the 1930s. At the far end of the gallery, in this photograph, can be seen a portrait of George IV as Prince of Wales, flanked by portraits of the first Marquis and Marchioness of Ormonde.

In 1645, the Supreme Council of the Catholic Confederation made the castle its seat receiving the Papal Nuncio there, but that body was dissolved by the Earl of Ormonde in 1648, acting as Charles I's representative.

The great scientist Robert Boyle, a founder member of the Royal Society and a descendant of Robert Boyle the great Earl of Cork, being a relative of the Ormondes, spent much of his childhood with them in Kilkenny Castle. Opposite to the castle, occupying what were the great stables is, today, the Kilkenny Design Centre, where much of the finest design work in Ireland is to be seen. The Castle, the Design Centre, St Canice's Cathedral, the Roth House and Kyteler's Inn are all very well worth visiting today, but in the middle of the last century a visit to the castle would have been restricted.

Waterford Railway Station and the Great Trestle Toll Bridge of 1794, C. 1865

A RAILWAY CONNECTION BETWEEN DUBLIN AND WATERFORD WAS established in 1854, but did not come as close to the city as the railway station seen in the photograph which was opened in September, 1864. From it our mid-eighteen-sixties' travellers would have taken an outside or inside car across the great trestle toll-bridge. It was built by the internationally famous Lemuel Cox, an American engineer who had gained great experience of spanning large rivers in his native country, enabling him to bridge some of the widest estuaries in Ireland so effectively that his bridges remained in use for many years. This trestle bridge, whose 832 feet made it the longest in Ireland, had two bascule spans at its centre which lifted to allow just enough room for a barque to pass into the upstream tidal water. This remarkable bridge survived into the twentieth century, being freed of toll in 1908 and replaced by the present bridge in 1912.

All these wooden trestle-bridges, built before the coming of railways, were intended as horse-carriage and foot-bridges only and though strengthened to take light motor vehicles in later years were of too light a construction to bear the weight of railway locomotives and loaded rolling-stock.

As can be well seen in the photograph, the City of Waterford developed along the south bank of the River Suir. Its situation naturally appealed strongly to the Vikings who settled here in the middle of the ninth century and made it into one of the most important ports of Ireland in their time. They developed the port and its defences for over three hundred years, enclosing the town with strong walls and defensive towers, some of which remain to this day, before the Anglo-Normans Strongbow, Earl of Pembroke, and Raymond le Gros, at the instigation of the English King Henry II, laid siege to and captured it in 1170, putting the Norse inhabitants to the sword. Aware of its great strategic importance, Strongbow at once rebuilt and strengthened its defences and to consolidate his gains married the Irish King of Leinster's daughter Aoife (Eva). To put a curb on Strongbow's rapidly growing power was one of the motives which brought King Henry II to Ireland, where he landed at Waterford on October 18th, 1171 and declared Waterford to be a Royal City. King John, when Lord of Ireland, and Richard II, when seeking support, both visited the City and increased its privileges. The townspeople of Waterford maintained a degree of loyalty to the English Crown which lasted until the English Civil War. Their refusal to admit the Pretenders Perkin Warbeck and Lambert Simnel was rewarded by Henry VII with the granting of the motto *Urbs intacta manet Waterfordia* which remains its motto today.

Reginald's Tower and The Quay, Waterford, C. 1865

One of the most interesting remains of Viking Waterford - the name comes from the Norse Vedrafjordr - is 'Reginald's Tower' at the junction of The Mall and The Quay, said to have been built in 1003 by Reginald the Norseman. It was one of the first of Waterford's defences to be re-built by Strongbow after his capture of the town. The building has played a varied part in the history of the city, its massive strength making it an important part of the defences and also leading, in 1463, to its use as a mint. In 1819 it was converted into a police-station and it now houses the small Civic Museum which is well worth a visit. In the back gardens of houses in the streets that run parallel to the original Viking built walls remains of these may be seen and several other Norse towers remain, though in re-edified form. Not far from Reginald's Tower is a small, old cemetery which has associated with it the only vampire legend to be found in Ireland, in which the vampire has been said to have the form of a beautiful woman.

The Quay has until very recently been the hub of Waterford's commercial life, but with the development of rail, road and air transport, its importance as a seaport has declined seriously, though it now has a recently opened airport. From 1824 to 1959 regular passenger steam-ship sailings to Pembrokeshire ports were maintained, except during the two World Wars, from Adelphi Quay (just behind the photographer). Changing from New Milford, in Milford Haven to Fishguard Harbour at Goodwick when the latter was completed in 1906. This service offered, in the 1950s, one of the most comfortable and enjoyable routes to the South West of Ireland. The atmosphere aboard the coal-burning turbine-steamer *Great Western*, was like that of a private club where many of the passengers were friends of one another. A good express train service from Paddington got one to Goodwick with plenty of time to settle into one's cabin on the boat before it sailed at midnight and steaming up the Suir for the last hour of the passage was one of the most pleasant introductions to Ireland that a passenger could desire.

In the mid 1860s Waterford was a flourishing port and the seat of many ship-owning families, but it is interesting to see how few services there were on The Quay, very primitive manually operated cranes and small iron-wheeled trucks for the use of the stevedores. The large, roughly-coopered barrels were not for the transportation of fluids, but were used as packaging for dry-goods, the period equivalent of our cardboard and expanded polystyrene packaging of today. On the one nearest to us a merchant's marks may be seen.

The Footway and Carriageway of Cox's Bridge and Waterford Railway Station, C. 1865

In the mid 1860s steam-ship passenger and goods services ran between Waterford, Bristol, Liverpool, and London, operated by the Waterford Steamship Company, whose principal was William Malcolmson, then also the Chairman of the Waterford and Limerick Railway Company.

These services, together with the service to New Milford with its express rail link to London, made Waterford Station one of the busiest in Ireland. Nearly a quarter of all the emigrants from Ireland during and after the great famine passed over Cox's bridge, the majority on their way as steerage passengers to Liverpool and London. The great bridge was constructed with a footway on either side and a carriageway in the middle, the footways being railed off by a substantial wooden barrier. It is interesting to notice that the carriageway was floored by planks running across the bridge while the raised footway was floored by planks running longitudinally. Delivery vans, carts and outside cars are waiting at the station for the arrival of the trains at what was then the longest railway station platform in Ireland, from which rail services ran to Dublin, Cork, Limerick, Killarney and Tralee, but Galway could still only be reached via Dublin. Many tourists from England in the mid 1860s would leave from this station for Cork and Killarney, but those wishing to see something of the south coast of Ireland would leave Waterford from Manor Street Station of the Waterford and Tramore Railway on the south side of the river.

This curious little seven-mile long railway, having only two stations, both termini, surprisingly turned out to be a profitable enterprise, maintaining its independence from its opening in 1853 until its incorporation into the Great Southern and Western Railway in 1925. Throughout its life it continued to employ some of the oldest locomotives and rolling-stock to be found in continuous use in Ireland.

Bathing-boxes on the Strand, Tramore, County Waterford

In the mid-nineteenth century on the strand of every 'watering-place', where 'mixed-bathing' took place, were to be found the 'bathing-boxes', then, and for a good number of years to come, considered essential to propriety and decorum. These curious contrivances seem to have originated in late Georgian times at Brighthelmstone, later shortened to Brighton, on the south coast of England, from where they spread rapidly to other seaside resorts and to the fashionable resorts along the northern coast of France, where they were known as cabines. These small wooden huts on wheels were individual changing-rooms in which members of either sex could strip and put on the elaborate and extensive bathing costumes of the day and then descend the wooden stairs to enter the water.

In the really fashionable resorts, such as Brighton, bathing-boxes took on their most elaborate form, having shafts so that they could be drawn in and out of the water by a horse, enabling their occupants to enter and leave them dry-shod and the steps were frequently screened on the sides and on top by a hood so that their bashful occupants could not be observed until they were immersed. On the more remote beaches, such as the one shown, the boxes were of much simpler and lighter construction so that they could be manhandled into and out of the water and, at the end of the season, drawn up out of the reach of storms.

The day appears to be a windless but overcast one, perhaps threatening rain, as early summer days frequently do in these parts, for the ladies walking along the stony upper beach are almost all carrying raised umbrellas and few, if any, of the bathing-boxes seem to be in use.

The Catholic church, on the extreme left of the photograph, the building of which was begun in 1856, appears to be almost completed, which enables us to date the photograph with a reasonable degree of accuracy, as work ceased on the building in 1871.

Tramore began to assume its character as a 'watering place' in the early 1850s and has maintained the status of a resort ever since, having a particularly fine strand on which the bathing-boxes are no longer to be seen! There are a number of interesting megalithic remains in the vicinity, passage graves, wedge graves and portal dolmens but all without any megalithic art.

As the railway comes to an end at Tramore, our travellers who wish to continue their tour along the south coast must now take to the roads on outside or inside cars to continue their journey westwards towards Dungarvan and then Youghal, where the wide estuary of the Blackwater has to be crossed by another long, trestle toll-bridge if a twenty-mile detour to Cappoquin is to be avoided.

The toll-bridge across the Blackwater estuary at Youghal, County Cork, C. 1867

THE WIDE RIVER ESTUARIES OF THE LARGE RIVERS OF THE SOUTH East of Ireland, the Slaney, the Suir and the Blackwater represented formidable barriers to coastal roads serving the area. Initially, these estuaries were crossed by ferries, but in the late eighteenth and early nineteenth centuries they were spanned by trestle-bridges built on piles, as the waters of the estuaries were too tidal to make boat-supported bridges a permanent practicality. The bridge over the Blackwater at Youghal was a much more rough and ready structure than Lemuel Cox's masterpiece at Waterford. It had no raised, protected footway and, being considerably narrower, pedestrians had to take their chances with the horse-drawn traffic as they crossed it. The photograph shows the arrangements for a small lifting span, but one of very restricted length, allowing only vessels of very narrow beam to pass into the upper estuary; never-the-less the bridge survived into the era of the motor car, though with modifications to its structure.

The Blackwater is one of the most famous of the Irish salmon-fishing rivers and along its banks are to be found many traditional recipes which do justice to this superb fish. Butter, cream and other dairy products form an important part of Irish cookery as they do in all the Celtic areas.

Bradán Bácáilte - Baked Salmon.

1 small salmon, cleaned and de-scaled
150ml dry white wine or dry cider
2 large sprigs of parsley
300ml double cream
3 heaped tablespoons of butter
juice of 1 lemon
salt and freshly ground white pepper

Trim the tail off the fish and stuff its gullet and interior with the parsley, grease an oven-proof dish with a little of the butter, place the fish in it and dot with the remainder of the butter. Season and pour the wine or cider around the fish, cover with a fitting lid or with foil and bake in an oven pre-heated to 180°C. (350°F.) Gas mark 4 for 15 minutes per 0.5Kg. weight of fish. After half an hour take from the oven, pour the cream over the fish and cover it again with the lid or with foil and return it to the oven to finish cooking. When cooked, remove the skin and any fins or side bones. Put the whole fish onto a warmed serving dish and keep hot. Reduce the sauce in the cooking dish on the top of the stove, add the lemon juice, re-check the seasoning, mix well and serve a little over the skinned fish and the remainder in a sauce boat.

Once across the Blackwater to Youghal, our tourists could resume their journey to Cork by rail on the Cork and Youghal Railway, completed in 1861.

The Imperial Hotel, The South Mall, Cork City, C. 1865

If, instead of taking the train from Youghal, our imaginary travellers had continued their journey to Cork by one of the Bianconi four-wheeled, two-horsed outside cars that the railways were fast replacing, they would have been brought to the Bianconi Car Office at the Imperial Hotel, at the corner of the South Mall and Parnell Street. This fine building has remained for well over a century one of the best hotels in Cork, although its dignified front has not been improved by some modernisation.

Cork City having been a particular prize for the many contending factions throughout the course of Irish history is rather more depleted in intact ancient buildings than other major Irish cities, but by the eighteenth century conditions were becoming more stable and this, the second in size of Irish cities, is rich in beautiful eighteenth-century houses, which have, in many cases, suffered less from modern disfigurement than many in Dublin, where some of the finest Irish Georgian terraces of a unique and distinguished style, have been swept away to make room for office blocks. When our travellers had settled in and come down to dinner, what might they have had as a main dish? Probably something like this:-

Mairteoil Ghalstofa le Leann Dubh - *Beefsteak Braised with Stout*

> 2 tablespoons beef dripping (or sunflower oil)
> 2 flat tablespoons seasoned flour
> 3 bay leaves
> 150ml. Murphy's Cork Stout
> 1.25 Kg. stewing beef, cubed
> salt and freshly milled black pepper
> 1 large onion, peeled, sliced
> 225g. carrots, scraped, sliced
> 12 whole black peppercorns
> 1 heaped tablespoon parsley, chopped

Make the fat or oil smoking hot in the bottom of a casserole and put the bay leaves and peppercorns in it, then seal and brown the beef cubes on all faces. Move them to the edge and put in the sliced onion, just allowing it to soften before stirring the beef cubes into it, then sprinkle with the seasoned flour and let all brown just a little before adding the stout and an equal amount of boiling water, check seasoning and adjust if needed, then add the sliced carrots, cover and bring back to the boil and braise, covered, in an oven pre-heated to 160°C. (325°F). Gas Mark 3 for 1 1/2 hours, checking to see that it is not getting too dry and adding a little stout if needed. Check that the beef is tender with a fork and give a little longer cooking if needed. Turn into a serving dish and sprinkle with the freshly chopped parsley.

Morrison's Island and Quay and the South Mall, Cork City, C. 1865

This is the view of Cork that our travellers would have seen as they left their hotel on the morning after their arrival. The name of the city comes from the Irish word for a marsh, corcach, for the River Lee formerly spread tentacles of water through the marshy ground hereabouts, forming small islands. On the slightly higher ground to the south west of this marsh, St.Finbar established an anchorite's hermitage in the early seventh century, around which a monastery of the Celtic Church grew until its wealth attracted Viking raiders in 820 and 838. The Vikings built a fort on one of the marshy islands in 846 and consolidated their position by forming a permanent trading settlement on a more ample basis in 917. It is from this Viking settlement that the City of Cork derives and the Vikings commercial use of the River Lee gave origin to the area's economic importance. It is interesting to note that the Scottish Clan Morrison is one of Viking origin and members of the family have left their name on what at one time was an island in this marsh. The schooner *Jamestown* of Waterford, lying at its mud berth by Morrison's Quay shows that these tentacles and backwaters of the Lee continued to be of importance to the commercial life of the City throughout the nineteenth century. It is intriguing to wonder what goods have just been discharged from her and loaded onto the cart which is just about to pull away, for this traffic reminds us that the railway network was not yet ready to compete for the carriage of freight with these coasters, a large number of which were built by the Tyrell family of Arklow. Schooners, small barques and Galway hookers all engaged in the coastal trade were only gradually replaced by steam in the late nineteenth and early twentieth centuries.

The large tidal rivers of most major Irish ports had not yet been augmented by basins with lock gates and pontoon docks so that the mud berth was still widely in use, requiring a long gang-plank so that the vessels could be berthed well away from the quay wall to avoid damage during the falling and rising tide. Besides the sailors and stevedores, small boys, many of them bare-footed have been drawn, as small boys still are, to watch the shipping in the port. By walking up the South Mall, our tourists would pass, by grand Parade into Patrick Street. All these main thoroughfares and the whole of the central part of the city were built over the drained marsh and even today not a few of the lower lying parts are sometimes subject to flooding when prolonged heavy rain, strong south-westerly gales and high tides occur together.

St Patrick's Street, Cork, with inside and outside cars, C. 1862

COUNTY CORK IS THE LARGEST OF THE IRISH COUNTIES AND CORK City's curving Patrick's Street was the main shopping centre for the area, as it still is today. Although the buildings have not changed so very greatly, the appearance of the traffic in the roadway is vastly different. Behind the outside car nearest to us are two inside cars of an unsophisticated type, having open rears, closed only by drawing a pair of waterproof curtains and having each only one small, unglazed opening to the front. The state of the main thoroughfare explains why the four-wheeled Brougham, drawn by only a single horse, is not yet to be seen in the city. The photograph is too early to show the horse-drawn tramways that were introduced in 1873. Unlike those already in existence in Dublin, they were not a success, being discontinued only three years later.

A good example of a Municipal gas-lamp standard is to be seen at the right, surmounting a public drinking-fountain where a man in a cut-away coat is refreshing himself Quite a number of the gas-lamp standards remain today, though converted to electric light. Just beyond it is a street 'crossing' of a rather different type from those seen in Dublin. At the centre of the photograph, a beggar sits near the edge of the pavement.

Crúibíní - Crubeens.

These are pigs' hind-feet. The fore-feet can also be used but they have more bone and less meat. They are still eaten in the country today, simply boiled for two hours with a carrot and an onion, thyme and sage and salt and pepper in the water, but to get the best out of them, after cooking they should be split, the meat taken off the bones when hot, allowed to get cold, then the pieces brushed with beaten egg and formed into rissoles with a coating of bread-crumbs and grilled and served hot with Michael Kelly's Sauce, made by mixing well together one flat tablespoon of raw cane sugar, and 1 flat teaspoonful each of dry English mustard-powder, freshly ground black pepper and 1 or two tablespoons of garlic vinegar (the last according to taste). When these are all thoroughly incorporated blend the mixture evenly into 1 cup of melted butter and serve with the hot grilled rissoles.

Michael Kelly, who was born in Cork around 1790, was an Irish composer who became Director of Music at the Theatre Royal, Drury Lane, London, in 1822.

A Vista of Cork from Audley Place, C.1862

As we saw, the city of Cork formed on the flat marshes to the south of the Lee, but the land to the north of the river is of a quite different character. Here it rises so steeply in places that the construction of south-north running streets can only be effected by resorting at times to steps, but it is interesting to note that the local pedestrians seem to prefer the steep incline to the steps provided by the Municipality even though the street is much too steep for wheeled traffic.

From Audley Place one has a magnificent view of the flat parts of the city beyond the Lee. The street is quite short and where the incline becomes more gentle, St Patrick's Hill begins, giving place in its turn to Bridge Street and St Patrick's Bridge leading over the Lee to St Patrick's Street which is seen bearing around to the left to join Grand Parade.

Cork has provided us with many distinguished painters, sculptors and architects as well as composers, novelists, playwrights and actors. The city has acquired a unique reputation in Ireland as centre of literature and witty conversation. Let us think of what might be served as a main course at a convivial dinner.

Uaineoil Rósta le Húlla   Roast Lamb with Apples

2 Kg. loin of lamb, boned
3 whole cloves
1 lemon, juice and grated zest of
1 level tablespoon of powdered ginger
0.5 Kg. cooking apples, peeled, sliced
salt and freshly milled black pepper
1 level tablespoon brown cane sugar
2 tablespoons of melted butter or sunflower oil
600ml. dry cider

Rub the joint inside and out with the lemon juice and grated zest. Lay the apple slices over the inner side of the joint, sprinkle with the sugar and the cloves and roll up tightly, secure and score the outside well, then rub all over with the ginger, salt and pepper, put the joint into a roasting tin and brush lightly all over with the melted butter or oil and roast in an oven pre-heated to 200°C. (400°F.) Gas Mark 6 for half an hour, then lower the heat to 180°C. (350°F.) Gas Mark 4 and continue roasting for a further hour and 20 minutes. Heat the cider to just below boiling and baste the joint at least three times during this last period of roasting. When done reserve the joint on a hot dish and keep hot while pouring the excess oil from the top of the roasting tin juices and reducing them on the hob at a high heat, seasoning and serving in a hot creamer with the joint. An excellent and simple *pièce de résistance!*

The Harbour Master's Office, Queenstown (now Cobh), Cork Harbour, C.1865

AFTER THE CORK STEAMER, *SIRIUS*, OPERATED BY THE CUNARD Company, left Cobh for America in 1838, to become the first steamship to cross the Atlantic, Cobh rapidly became Ireland's main transatlantic port. Until almost the end of the nineteenth century, most transatlantic liners were of such size that they could use the sheltered waters of the harbour, coming to anchor while their passengers were transferred to them from the quayside by tenders. The little town of Cobh - it was renamed 'Queenstown' after Queen Victoria landed there in 1849, but reverted again to its original name in 1922 - has a unique maritime tradition going back to the year 1720, for it was then, at Cobh, that the very first yacht-club in the world was founded by Lord Cloncurry, preceding even the Royal Yacht Squadron at Cowes on the Isle of Wight. At first it was called The Water Club, but soon became the Royal Cork Yacht Club, the name that it keeps to this day.

It is hardly surprising that this development took place where it did, for the whole of the south west coast of Ireland is a magnificent cruising ground which has brought yachtsmen from all over the world into its waters for over two centuries and the world famous Royal Cork Yacht Club has played a large part in promoting that energetic sport. A more ideal venue than Cork Harbour could not be found, one which has not yet been overtaken by the congestion of industrial traffic such as that which now affects the Solent and Southampton Water and even the English Channel itself. Cork Harbour and the waters that extend beyond it to the west are still comparatively unencumbered, while the variety of sailing possible on this diversified and well lit coast provides sport for all from the ocean racer to the 14-foot week-ender. The extensive waters of the harbour and Loch Mahon form a wonderful ground for gaining experience and confidence before venturing out beyond Forts Camden and Carlisle which guard the entrance to the open ocean and, in the winding creeks and off wooded promontories such as Currabinny, many safe anchorages are available near to which, in adjacent old houses, small colonies of lovers of the sport have formed. It is hardly possible for anyone who does not love the sea fully to understand the enchantment of Cork Harbour.

Cork Harbour, the guardship and Spike and Haulbowline Islands, C. 1862

The large natural harbour of Cork, is, with that of Sydney in Australia, one of the most attractive in the world. Its advantages as a safe haven for shipping has made it a centre of maritime endeavour from ancient times. Gentle hills and woodlands falling to the sheltered waters have been admired by countless travellers, including our supposed tourists of the 1860s.

Even today, when this charm has been eroded in places by industrial development, the main stretches and creeks of the great land-locked bay remain unspoilt. None of this industrialization was in place in the 1860s, though the British Navy had made, on Hawlbowline Island, the tip of which is seen on the right, their naval base for the South Atlantic Squadron and built on it extensive storage facilities, a naval barracks and a large isolation hospital in which to treat sailors and officers suffering from tropical fevers. The other and larger island of Spike had built upon it a strong fort and a prison, in which were confined political and other prisoners awaiting transportation to the Australian and Tasmanian Colonies. In the mid 1850s, the Admiralty decided to have a number of graving docks built on Haulbowline for the maintenance of naval vessels and a Civil Service decision was made that this should be effected by using the labour of the prisoners. To facilitate this a long pile bridge was constructed from the end of the pier on Spike to the nearest part of Haulbowline. Daily, across this narrow bridge seen in the photograph, the gangs of prisoners trudged to work and back again to the prison in the evening. The scheme, however, was a failure. So inefficient was the convict labour that, in the 1870s, with still a major part of the work incomplete, it was given up and contract labour employed, by which the work was quickly finished.

Even by the 1860s the big Atlantic liners had become too large to use docks in the harbour without the danger of grounding, so passengers were brought out to them as they anchored off the mouth by tenders, mostly departing from Passage or Queenstown.

This beautiful harbour was the last sight of Ireland not only for the prisoners but for many of those emigrating to the New World after the great famine of 1844 to 1849 and for many years after that. So extensive is this sheltered water that it was more economic in the 1860s and 1870s to supply the communities around its shores by small steamers than to use horse transport on the roads and these steamers had comfortable accommodation to enable tourists to enjoy daily cruises around the harbour and visits to the different resorts on its shores such as Monkstown, Queenstown, where Queen Victoria landed in 1849, formerly and now Cobh (Cove) and Crosshaven. These steamers ran a regular scheduled service from the very heart of the city itself.

The Paddle-Steamer Lee *loading at St. Patrick's Quay, Cork, C.1868*

The remarkable service of inshore steamer transport that Cork Harbour enjoyed throughout most of the nineteenth century was begun by individual vessels as early as 1813. The first company fleet to work this area in the early 1840s was that of the Clyde shipbuilders Tod and McGregor. These vessels were taken over by the Citizen's River Steamer Company, which was founded in 1844 and lasted until 1890. The C.R.S.C. took possession of P.S. *Lee* and her sister ship P.S. *Citizen* in 1861. Both were built on the Clyde, having iron hulls 160 feet in length and single-expansion steam-engines. They continued to work for the Company until its closure in 1890, carrying passengers and a wide variety of goods as may be seen in the photograph. Beer and flour are the chief items seen here, together with dry-goods in the characteristic roughly-coopered barrels, but newspapers too were a not unimportant item as well as potatoes and other vegetables.

It appears to be a fine day, as a number of passengers have already taken their seats on the upper deck, but these vessels were equipped with quite a sizeable cabin in which both food and drink were available. This service offered to the visitor the best possible way of enjoying one of the most pleasant and extensive natural harbours in Europe.

Until the arrival of the large roll-on roll-off ferries of recent years, the passenger cross-channel steamers were able to sail right up the Lee and berth as near to the city centre as Penrose Quay, and it was here that the St George's Steam Packet Company established its headquarters in 1821. Although it became one of the largest shipping companies of the early nineteenth century, it was never strong financially and its southern Irish interests were vested in a new shipping company, the Cork Steam Ship Company, formed by Ebenezer Pike, a prominent Cork business tycoon, in 1843. The fine Georgian building of the St George's Steam Packet Company becoming the headquarters of the new Company. For those easily affected by the motion of boats, a crisp, fresh-tasting little biscuit to nibble at is often of help.

Brioscaí Liomóide - Lemon Biscuits

100g. butter
grated zest of 1 lemon
3 heaped tablespoons of white caster sugar
juice of 1 lemon
175g. white plain flour
1 small egg, well beaten

Cream the butter and sugar together until light, then add the flour, the lemon zest, the juice and lastly, the beaten egg. Mix thoroughly and then leave standing for one hour, then grease some baking sheets and drop small spoonfuls of the mixture onto them, well separated from one another. Bake in an oven pre-heated to 180°C. (350°F.) Gas Mark 4 for 15 minutes only and lift from the baking sheets with a slice while still hot, placing them on a wire rack to cool before keeping them in an air-tight tin..

Penrose Quay, Cork, with the St George's Steam-Packet Company's Building, C. 1870

As its name suggests, this early steam-packet company began its life, in 1821, by operating services mainly across the St George's Channel, but grew to be one of the largest shipping firms in the world in the early part of the century. It's House Flag consisted of a St George's Cross on a white ground and this was the occasion of much friction with the British Admiralty and individual British Admirals, for the conventions of the British Navy require an Admiral to fly a St George's Cross as an indication of his flagship. Quite a few Admirals, sometimes overseas, on seeing a meer merchant vessel flying the undefaced St George's Cross at the mast-head would send peremptory signals to the Company's vessels to strike the flag at once. This was always politely refused until, after an incident in the Persian Gulf, the Company agreed to alter its House Flag to a St George's Cross on a white ground defaced by a blue star at the centre, as a means of placating the Lords of Admiralty!

When Ebenezer Pike took over the local interests of the original company in 1843, he established the offices of the Cork Steam Ship Company in the fine old building and build the new company into a powerful one engaging in many cross-channel services and also engaging largely in the deep-water trade world-wide. A paddle-steamer cargo vessel is seen alongside Penrose Quay, reminding us that the diverse trade carried out by this company made it so successful that, in 1871 the Company was split into two, one continuing the many cross-channel services while the other took over the deep-water cargo side of the business.

At Cork, many more tourists might be expected to join our party as the service from New Milford in Milford Haven, with its express train service to Paddington was a very popular route to the south west of Ireland, as it continued to be right up to the second half of this century. Edith Somerville gives an amusing account of a journey from London by this route in 1899 in *Through Connemara in a Governess Cart*. The effect of the cooking smells from the supper being prepared for famished passengers on the S.S. *Inisfallen* is mentioned in a way that leads one to believe that catering on the cross-channel services of the 1890s left something to be desired. When our travellers have seen the undoubted charms of this locality, a great many of them would entrain for that most famous of all Irish beauty-spots, which, even today, draws a round the year crowd of visitors, Killarney.

Two gentlemen about to set out on a fishing-trip. The Lake Hotel, Killarney, C. 1865

KILLARNEY HAD DRAWN VISITORS IN NUMBERS FROM THE eigheenth century onwards by its combination of startlingly picturesque groupings of mountains, lakes and woodlands and the variety of sport to be had there. Already, in the early 1800s it had become a resort and was in full expansion by the time William Makepeace Thackeray visited it in 1842 while writing *The Irish Sketchbook*. By the 1860s the inns and lodging-houses had been overtaken by the growth of hotels and one of the most delightful in Ireland was already well established. Lucky indeed would have been our travellers if they had secured accommodation here, for its situation, on a bay of Lough Leane, looking across the water towards Tomies and Purple Mountain, is one of the most attractive of any hotel in Ireland. Many visitors came here to fish as well as for the extraordinary delight of being rowed about the lakes past tree-covered islands. A race-course was opened near the town and regattas on Lough Leane were a regular feature in Thackeray's time, as they are at the present day, drawing large crowds. In *The Irish Sketchbook* he gives us a brief description of a 'Race Ordinary' or Table d'Hôte dinner during a race week: '. . . for a sum of twelve shillings, any man could take his share of turbot, salmon, venison and beef, with port and sherry and whisky [sic*] punch at discretion.' We are bound to reflect (page 12) that there were occasions when this last observation was forgotten by the distinguished author. The exterior of the delightful Lake Hotel still appears much as it did in the 1860s but a large wall of plate glass has been built into the restaurant giving an overwhelming view of the sunset reflected in the waters of the lake as one goes in to dinner.

The mild winter climate of Kerry, occasioned by the Gulf Stream flowing on two sides of the county, gives a lushness and variety to the flora. Delicate plants can flourish there, particularly around Killarney where the mountains shelter the low lying ground from the Atlantic gales. *Arbutus unedo*, the Strawberry Tree is one of the most spectacular, apearing in great numbers in the woods surrounding the lakes and growing to unusual size. Woodland walks are made delightful by the number of waterfalls and streams, in sheltered clefts near which one can still come across the Killarney Fern, *Trichomanes redicans* as well as the impressive and decorative *Osmundum regalis*. Common at the time when this photograph was taken, both are now harder to find due to the depredations of increasing numbers of tourists.

*Thackeray here follows the Anglicised Scottish (and English) spelling 'whisky' for the potation, the expression for which in the original Gaelic is 'uisce beatha' or 'water of life' In Ireland the custom is to include an e - 'whiskey'.

A guide shows an artistic visitor the 'Friar's Grave' on Inisfallen, Killarney, C.1855

The island of Inisfallen on Lough Leane, a half mile north west of Ross Castle, was regarded as one of the most beautiful on the lakes. In the sixth century, St Finan the Leper settled there and founded a monastery which grew to be one of the most important centres of learning in Ireland from the eleventh to the thirteenth century, during which period parts of the famous *Annals of Inisfallen* were written there, a solitary, incomplete copy of which survives in the Bodleian Library at Oxford. In 1320, the rules of the Benedictine Order were assumed by the monks and the monastery was enlarged. Though none of these later buildings survived intact, there is a little church or oratory, perched on the edge of a low cliff overlooking the lake which has a most beautiful Irish Romanesque doorway, well worth visiting the island to see.

Having been, for so long, a centre of tourism, Killarney and its surroundings have acquired an extensive accretion of false traditions and folklore, such as the fantasies spun around the 'Colleen Bawn', transported from the coast of Clare, and the escapades of the O'Donohues, produced for much the same reasons as the Capresi produced their stories and traditions of the Emperor Tiberius; in order to enthral the less well informed tourists, although among these heterogeneous offerings there are undoubtedly some that have a respectable antiquity and possibly commemorate real events now gilded by the patina of centuries. What the guide is showing the artist with his sketching materials may indeed be a grave, and indeed even that of a friar.

One thing that these photographs of the West of Ireland do show is the de-population produced by the famine and emigration. In 1842, when Thackeray passed through, everywhere he finds a seething population and crowds surrounding tourists as they do in Third World countries today. In Killarney, one would hardly have stepped ashore when people would have begun to appear from every direction. 'Strange savage faces might be seen peering from out of the trees; long-haired bare-legged girls came down the hill; some with green apples and very sickly-looking plums; some with whisky and goat's-milk : a ragged boy had a pair of stag's horns to sell : the place swarmed with people.' The famine came to an end in 1849, the emigration went on. The photographs of the mid 1860s show a picture very different from that described in *The Irish Sketchbook*. Killarney has always catered for a wide variety of visitors, ranging from those who prefer to relax and be transported about, by water or by road, to those who enjoy viewing landscapes or antiquities or those who are looking for sport and more energetic activities; for the latter a trek through the Gap of Dunloe provided then, as it does today, an ideal excursion.

A tourist bargains for a drink in the Gap of Dunloe, C. 1865

As one looks across Lough Leane from the restaurant of the Lake Hotel one sees, just as one would have done in the 1860s, Tomies and Purple Mountains. They are separated from the rest of the Magillicuddy's Reeks (pronounced Macklecuddy) Range by a deep, tortuous and narrow cleft; the Gap of Dunloe. Here, for four miles, one may walk, on a rough track taking one through the most impressive ravine in Ireland, until the Upper Lake of Killarney is reached. This was a very popular excursion in the 1860s and donkeys were available for the ladies outside Kate Kearney's Cottage, near the start of the Gap, a house of refreshment commemorating a local beauty of the eighteenth century. The ascending gradient and the roughness of the road are known to arouse a thirst in travellers and the narrowness of the way making interception easy, it has always been a popular spot for offering stimulants and souvenirs. A close inspection suggests that the bottle is one of brandy rather than whiskey, which indicates a changing fashion from Thackeray's time. There are many places in the defile where complex echoes can be produced and the guides, then as now, encourage tourists to make their best efforts to awaken them. Let's hope that the refreshment enjoyed by our traveller put him in good voice. About a mile from the head of the Gap the Black Lough is reached. Here, it is claimed, St Patrick drowned the last snake in Ireland.

Probably it was not a water snake, but of whatever variety, tradition asserts that its venom has left the lakelet inimical to fish-life since the incident! In the times of the photograph our travellers would have found boats waiting in the Upper Lake to take them, by the natural waterway called The Long Range, through rapids running under Old Weir Bridge, into either the Middle or Muckross Lake or into Lough Leane and so back to their hotel where, in preparation for extending their tour of Kerry, a substantial dinner is recommended.

Breac - Trout.
Fried Brown Trout.

If you are lucky enough to be able to get some of these altogether delicious little fish of the mountain streams really fresh, then the most perfect way of cooking them is also quite the simplest. Behead, clean and wash them, then let them rest for half an hour in lightly salted water. Take them out, pat them dry with kitchen paper or a cloth and put them into a pan of melted butter that is just about to turn brown. Cook them as short a time as possible, but just before you lift them onto a hot dish, sprinkle them with a few drops of lemon juice, place them on their dish, pour the pan juices over them and *serve at once!*

A Kerry farmer and his family, C. 1870

THE RING OF KERRY, A TRIP FROM KILLARNEY AROUND THE Iveragh Peninsula and back to Killarney again can now easily be done in a day but needed three in the mid-nineteenth century. By 1870, the County was beginning to recover from the most terrible effects of famine and depopulation. Never a rich, productive agricultural area, in places little pockets of fertile soil gave rise to small farming communities among the mountains. Our visitors, on the way to the coast, would have seen, in areas sheltered from the wind, in valleys with a fertile soil, small farms such as this one, in front of which the farmer, his wife and their nine children are seen and another is clearly on the way. A little farm in the foothills of the Magillicuddy's Reeks, seen in the background, the highest peak of which, Carrantuohill, at 3414 feet is the highest mountain in Ireland. Built onto the end of the cottage which is nearest to us is the byre for the animals, perhaps a few little Kerry cows, a small breed giving a rich sweet milk. A young pig is seen approaching the door of the byre. The cottage is well thatched, the byre more roughly so, but the house has two chimneys indicating that it had two fireplaces and this may indicate two cottages.

A wooden tub, sunk in the ground, is outside one door and a small well is seen let into the drystone wall of the field across the road. Although the younger children are bare-footed, the farmer, his wife and the children are relatively well dressed, but his eldest son appears to have lost his right arm.

The stony nature of the soil on the hillside with many outcrops of rock has been improved in places by building terraces of drystone walling and infilling with fertile soil, even so, with all the effort that this clearly hardworking family can do, there is still only a very thin living to be made on their diminutive holding, though this might be augmented by keeping sheep on the higher ground. Clearly, every resource has been employed to gain a living at a time when no hill farming subsidies were known. The number and condition of the trees show us that the valley situation is a sheltered one, as it would need to be on a peninsula that juts out into the Atlantic, but the Gulf Stream, then, as ever our greatest friend, keeps us in the temperate zone and the warm moisture-laden air produces a grass crop which more arid regions could not support on such rocky ground where the soil is a rich but thin skin on the rough face of the mountain.

Fishermen and curraghs, Ballinskelligs, County Kerry, C.1865

THE RING OF KERRY BRINGS ONE PAST A SUCCESSION OF headlands, cliffs and bays as fine as may be seen anywhere on the north west coast of Europe, the vistas of the ocean diversified by off-shore rocks and islands breaking the monotony of the horizon, both coast and islands having a variety of antiquities from Neolithic, Iron Age and Early Christian times. Close to the shore, except in mountain-sheltered bays and river valleys, the Atlantic gales have swept the landscape bare of trees and those that remain form living wind-vanes registering the direction of the prevailing sou' westerlies.

The small, rock-bound farms have made many of the farmers into fishermen, a mixed farming and fishing economy that has existed from Neolithic times.

The curragh, four of which are seen here, is a very ancient form of boat which has evolved from primitive Mesolithic vessels of coracle form. Until the appearance of canvas, the light, stressed-wood structure was covered with the tensed, tanned hides of animals, usually cattle, producing boats of extraordinary seaworthiness and durability, which by the ninth century had attained such a size that twenty or thirty persons could be taken aboard. These large curraghs, fitted with sails, made ocean voyages comparable in every way to those of the clinker-built ships of the Vikings. Soon after its introduction, it was found that, made waterproof with tar, canvas could be used in place of the more difficult to prepare and therefore more expensive hides.

Fishermen all around the coast of Ireland have always been glad to supplement their income by providing boat trips for tourists and these men are clearly ready to do the same. An excursion in a curragh, when handled by a skilled boatman, is a really delightful experience and can be a thrilling one. The curragh rides like a bubble on the surface of the water. It can be spun round, this way or that, in a second. It meets the seas joyfully, lifting over their tops with a seemingly effortless ease and appears to accommodate itself to the shapes of the water, but don't be deceived, this is also a demonstration of the experienced, specialized skill of an accomplished boatman and it is most unwise for anyone unused to these exceptional boats to attempt to venture out without a skilled man in charge!

To the left of the photograph are stacks of kelp, harvested from the rocks at low tide, drying before being burnt in a peat fire in a trench cut in the ground. As in the west of Scotland, the kelp industry began in the eighteenth century as a source of alkali. When cheaper ways of producing alkali were discovered it went into decline, to be revived in the succeeding century as a source of iodine, once again to decline and to be revived yet again in this century, as a source of alginates.

'Derrynane', the Home of Daniel O'Connell, County Kerry, C.1850

THE RT. HON. DANIEL O'CONNELL, M.P., THE LIBERATOR was one of the most important Irish political figures of the first half of the nineteenth century. No Irishman will need to be told about his indefatigable work in the cause of Catholic Emancipation, work to which he so devoted himself as to shorten his life. He remained, throughout, surrounded by his Kerry constituents and his family, to this day has an honourable place in the life of the County and his home has become a museum which is visited by thousands annually, though it was private at the time when this photograph was taken. Just after the Second World War, the house had fallen into a state of dilapidation, but funds were found for its restoration and a number of Irish literary figures with the necessary skills, devoted their time to the work, among them, Brendan and Dominic Behan.

'The Liberator' was a sportsman, known for his hospitality and the liberality of his table, so it is perhaps fitting to include here an excellent regional recipe.

Oiseoil Rósta - Roast Venison

For the marinade:-

75cl red wine
large sprig of rosemary
1 medium onion or 3 shallots, peeled and sliced
3 bay leaves
8 crushed juniper berries (4 if fresh)
1 small sprig thyme
4 tablespoons olive oil
salt and freshly ground black pepper

The joint of venison should be left in the marinade, in a cool room, for at least 24 hours, being turned at least three times during that period. Then remove it, reserving the marinade, pat the joint dry with kitchen paper and lard it well over the sides and top with plenty of streaky bacon rashers, while the oven is being pre-heated to 220°C. (375°F.) Gas Mark 5. When the oven is at the correct temperature put in the larded joint and roast for a period of 20 minutes to the 0.5Kg, basting often. Reduce the marinade on the top of the stove and when roasting time is half completed, pour two cups of the hot marinade over the joint, repeating this twenty minutes before cooking time has elapsed. Season the remaining marinade and serve hot in a sauce-boat with the joint.

The West Gate, Clonmell, County Tipperary, C. 1865

To reach 'Cashel of the Kings' after their 'Ring of Kerry' tour, our travellers would have gone by rail (via Limerick Junction) to Clonmell, there to get a Bianconi car to Cashel. Clonmell, the largest town in County Tipperary, was once a walled city. The Catholic Confederacy had its seat here in 1641 and during Cromwell's siege of 1650, defended by Hugh Dubh O'Neill and 1250 Ulster troops, the city offered the stiffest resistance of any that he had besieged either in England or Ireland. Clonmell can claim to have given us some of the most distinguished Jesuit scholars of the seventeenth century notably Fathers Thomas and Stephen White.

In 1713, it was the birthplace of Lawrence Sterne, author of *Tristram Shandy*, here too the writer George Borrow spent a short part of his childhood, beginning his study of Gaelic, to which he was introduced by a school friend while attending the Grammar School, a few yards from where the photograph was taken. He afterwards said that his interest in languages, which had such a formative influence on his development as a writer, was awakened here.

But it is a poor itinerant Italian vendor of cheap pictures, Carlo Bianconi, who would have been responsible for bringing our party to Clonmell. Arriving there in the early years of the century, he observed that there was no form of public transport within the financial reach of ordinary people. The rich had their own carriages or could hire them when they needed them and the main coaching lines only served towns along their routes and did not have the carrying capacity to give an adequate public service at fares that the majority of people could afford. He saved enough to buy an outside car and started a service between Clonmell and Cahir in 1817 The demand for the service was so great that very soon he had opened services to Tipperary and Cashel. Within a few years he established a service of large outside cars extending throughout twenty-three Irish Counties, efficient enough to be able to compete for many years with the growing railway network. Charles Bianconi ended his days a rich man.

The Gaelic name for Clonmell is Cluain Meala, meaning either 'Mel's meadow' or ' The Meadow of Honey'. The country surrounding the town is still the chief centre of honey production in Ireland.

Cúr Meala - Honey Cream

Take 450g. of liquid heather honey and separate the whites and yolks of four eggs. Beat the yolks into the honey and cook the mixture over hot water in a double boiler, but do not allow it to come to the boil, stirring continuously until it thickens, then allow it to cool, whisk the whites of the eggs until stiff, then fold them into the thickened honey and egg-yolk mixture until it is homogenous, pour into coupes and chill before serving.

Hore Abbey and the Rock of Cashel, County Tipperary, C.1865

FIFTEEN MILES FROM CLONMELL BY BIANCONI CAR BRINGS OUR party of tourists to 'Cashel of the Kings'. A 300-foot limestone rock rearing abruptly from a gently undulating plain. Though this eminence was probably a strong point from ancient times, the first record of fortification goes back to the early fifth century when Conall Corc and his followers who had, in previous generations, established a colony in Wales, returned to Ireland and captured the fertile surrounding lands while on the Rock itself Conall built a stone fort, in Gaelic, Cáiseal. This word, imported into Irish from the Latin Castellum, suggests the degree of Romanising influence to which the leaders of the Eóghanachta had been exposed during their period in Wales. It was while preaching within this stone enclosure that tradition asserts St Patrick used the simile of the clover-leaf to illustrate the idea of the Trinity. The kings of Cashel tended to have a closer association with the Church than many other Irish Royal dynasties. Two of their number were simultaneously both king and bishop.

Soon after 944, the Vikings captured Cashel but were defeated and ejected by the Dál Chais brothers, Mahon and Brian Boru and when, in 976, the former was murdered, Brian made himself King of Cashel and later High King of Ireland, only to fall victim to the Norsemen at the Battle of Clontarf in 1014. The O'Brian dynasty though retaining the title of Kings of Cashel, did not rule from there but in 1101, King Muirechertach donated Cashel to the Church to become the archiepiscopal see for the whole of Munster. Between 1127 and 1134, Cormac Mac Carthy, King of Desmond embellished the Rock with one of the finest Irish Romanesque buildings in the whole of the island, a miniature cathedral of the most beautiful design and ornamentation. But soon the history of the Rock was to darken. In 1171, King Henry II of England attended a National Synod where, in confirmation of a Papal Bull, the English king was acknowledged Lord of Ireland and thereafter much of the history of the Rock becomes a tale of arson and rapine extending from the fifteenth to the eighteenth centuries, in which it has to be admitted that the worst excesses were committed by Irishmen, both Catholic and Protestant.

Cashel has always attracted artists. We may easily imagine we see here one of our party at work on a sketch of Hore Abbey, a Benedictine off-shoot of Mellifont. The unfortunate Benedictines being summarily ejected by Archbishop Mac Carville in 1272, to be replaced by Cistercians, because, it is said, he dreamed that they were about to behead him.

To the right, in the distance, is the Rock itself and so rich is it in architectural treasures that not less than a day should be allowed in exploration and enjoyment.

Salmon Fishermen dry their nets by the Treaty Stone, Limerick

After their visit to Cashel, our party come to another city founded by the Vikings; Limerick. Arriving in 831, the Norsemen occupied in 927 an island in the Shannon, Inis Ubhdain, and founded there an important trading town. In 967, King Mahon of Thomond and his brother Brian Boru drove the Vikings out, burning and destroying the existing town but subsequently redeveloping it as a trading centre in which Viking life and trade continued, for Hrafn, a contemporary and friend of Ari the Learned, author of the *Islendingabók*, was a prosperous Viking merchant of Limerick. A later Thomond King who became High King of Ireland made the town his Royal Seat and his grandson styled himself *Rex Limricensis* Raymond le Gros captured the city in 1175. From now on Limerick became a prize contended for between the Kings of Thomond and the Anglo-Normans, the latter eventually gaining the upper hand. Prince (later King) John granted Limerick its first Royal Charter in 1197 and soon after, the Norsemen were driven out, to settle outside the walls. The people of Limerick supported their status as a Royal Chartered City even during several incursions when first Edward Bruce's forces and later the MacNamaras briefly occupied the town, until, in 1642 the city was captured by the army of the Catholic Confederacy, who held it for ten years until the Cromwell's army under Ireton stormed it, Ireton dying of plague within its walls. The most famous of the many sieges of the city was when the army of William III invested it in 1690 and during which it was so ably defended by Patrick Sarsfield and Hugh O'Neill. The terms of surrender, incorporated in the Treaty of Limerick, signed the following year on the stone seen in the photograph, were soon dishonoured and many were executed who had been promised their lives; thus the stone became a memorial to treachery.

To the right of the photograph, fishermen can be seen beside their nets which have been draped over the wall to dry. The netting of salmon was practised in the very heart of the city for a little up stream of this the salmon weir and fish traps were a concession which had formerly been a prerogative of the Bishop of Limerick but had by this time had passed into private hands.

The Shannon, the largest river of these islands, was a prodigious source of these splendid fish, so that, when the great hydro-electric power-station at Ard na Crusha came to be built, special provision had to be made to allow the fish to by pass the works to conserve the stocks in the long upper reaches of the river and which has effectively preserved the fish stocks to this day, enabling hundreds of miles of fly fishing to continue and bringing many salmon fishermen to Ireland every year.

Sarsfield Bridge and the statue of Viscount FitzGibbon

On their way to Galway, our group would most likely have spent a few days enjoying the spectacular cliff scenery of the coast of County Clare, basing themselves at the little spa of Lisdoonvarna. On their way there they would have crossed the Shannon by Sarsfield Bridge, which now commemorates by its name the brave defender of Limerick. Our travellers, looking to the left, would have seen on a plinth the bronze statue of a young hussar, flanked by two cannon. It was a memorial to Viscount FitzGibbon of the 8th Hussars, missing after the Charge of the Light Brigade at the battle of Balaclava. Dating from 1857, it was one of the sculptor Macdowall's most spirited works. The cannon are captured Russian guns. It is said that in the regiment a story survives that, many years after the Crimean War, when on duty near the North West Frontier, an old English-speaking man in worn clothing was invited to dinner. He aroused much curiosity by a perfect familiarity with the traditions of the regiment and of the mess, so much so that, after his departure, the Regimental Records were consulted and it was found that the only unaccounted for member of the right age was Viscount FitzGibbon. But the mysterious guest had vanished into the night. Rudyard Kipling's short story *The Man Who Was* is said to have been based on this incident. This fine work of Macdowall's has vanished too, for Viscount FitzGibbon was the great-grandson of 'Black-Jack' FitzGibbon, 1st. Earl of Clare and Lord Chancellor of Ireland, who was active in the suppression of the Rebellion of 1798 and did more than any man to bring about the Union with Great Britain and who has, consequently, remained one of the demonised figures of Irish popular history. Viscount FitzGibbon's statue was blown up in the early 1920s and the pieces flung into the Shannon, from which a few parts have been recovered, including the fine *basso-relievo* bronze plaque which shows an admirable depiction of the famous charge. It is now in the Limerick Museum. The plinth is now occupied by a memorial to the members of the I.R.A. who lost their lives in the fight for Irish independence, a bronze, begun by Albert Power and completed by his son, which has dignity, but nothing like the verve and finesse of Macdowall's splendid work. The politically motivated assassination of statuary is a mark of political immaturity wherever it may be perpetrated.

A picnic by the Pump House, Lisdoonvarna, County Clare, C. 1870

A BETTER BASE FOR ENJOYING THE NORTH CLARE CLIFF SCENERY and the curious Karst Limestone tract of the Burren could not be found either today or in the last century than the small spa of Lisdoonvarna. It has been popular for over two centuries for its sulphur and its chalybeate springs. The main spring, which goes by the name of the Gowlaun, is the sulphur one. Our tourists, after taking the waters at the pump room, have settled down to enjoy a picnic lunch. The two other medicinal springs are the Twin Wells containing iron and sulphur and the Rathbawn which has iron with a trace of manganese. Not far off is a small hot spring, the only one in Ireland.

Lisdoonvarna has another attraction. Every year for around a couple of centuries, after the harvest is in, Irishmen and Irishwomen from Ireland and abroad come to the spa in search of matrimony. This lends to the early autumn at the spa an especial atmosphere of cheerfulness and gallantry which is genuinely infectious and fun.

In the afternoon, an easy drive of seven miles by side-car to the south west, will bring our travellers to the top of the most spectacular sheer-faced cliffs in Ireland, the Cliffs of Moher. Moher is not somebody's name, but comes from the Gaelic word mothair, meaning a promontory fort, thus the name is really The Cliffs of the Fort, for an Iron Age fort once stood on the Hag's Head. All along this part of the west coast, to Loop Head and beyond, there exists a deeply embedded folk tradition that a large tract of land containing a town or village was suddenly engulfed by the sea.

On the way to Galway, the next day, our party would have been wise to travel via the Burren, to see something of its strange limestone terraces set here and there with Iron Age stone forts. In the spring the Karst benches and grykes are a mass of colourful wild flowers, including rare orchids and under these hills of North Clare are some of the most extensive caves in the country. In the last century most of these were unknown, but quite a few have now been explored by pot-holers and well mapped, drawing those experienced in the sport to these parts. It is unwise however for inexperienced solitary individuals to venture down, though, the proprietors of Ballygowan mineral water have opened a section of caves to the public which are easy to access. Descending then to sea level by the Corkscrew Hill, our tourists would drive around Galway Bay arriving in the evening, though from 1872 onwards, in the summer, they could have embarked on the paddle-steamer *Citie of the Tribes* at Ballyvaughan and enjoyed a direct crossing of the bay to arrive in the afternoon.

The Paddle-Steamer Citie of the Tribes *at anchor, Galway, 1872*

THE PADDLE-STEAMER TUG-BOAT *CITIE OF THE TRIBES* WAS BUILT for the Galway Bay Steam-Boat Company at South Shields in 1872 and began working from Galway in the summer of that year. Designed as a tug, and used as such, she was better known for opening the return passenger service across Galway Bay between Galway and Ballyvaughan in County Clare, the Midland Great Western Railway issuing through tickets from Dublin to Ballyvaughan where she also picked up passengers coming, like our party, from Lisdoonvarna Spa and other parts of Clare. Her hull was of iron and she had a single-expansion steam-engine Later on, in 1891, under the same owners she opened the first steam-boat service to the Aran Islands and continued on, without any mishaps, until 1903, when she was sold to other owners. The day is clearly a flat calm and our touring party will have enjoyed their crossing of the bay with its fine views of Black Head in Clare and the Connemara coast as they approached Galway. No food was available on board so our group would have done well to have brought a snack with them.

Rollóga Gíosta Prátaí - *Potato Yeast Rolls.*

100g. potatoes, peeled
1 teaspoonful of salt
25g, fresh or 15g. dried yeast
50g. butter
50g. sugar
50ml. warmed milk
450g. sifted plain white flour, warm
1 well beaten egg
A little milk for glazing
150ml. tepid water

Cook the potatoes in salted water and drain, keeping two tablespoons of the cooking liquid. Mash the potatoes exceedingly carefully and pass through a fine sieve into a bowl and keep warm. Cream the yeast in a bowl with the reserved two tablespoons of the cooking liquid, which should not be more than tepid and a level teaspoonful of the sugar, mix well to dissolve all the sugar and watch that it froths if it does not the yeast is dead. Sift the flour into a large mixing bowl, gradually adding the teaspoonful of salt so as to ensure an even mix. Make a well in the centre and add the remaining sugar and the mashed potatoes and mix thoroughly. Mix together in a warm jug the tepid milk and water and add the working yeast to this stirring well, then add the contents of the jug to the mixture in the bowl stirring well and then mix in the beaten egg. Knead the mixture well and then cover and leave, covered, in a warm place for half an hour or until the mass has doubled in size, then turn out onto a floured surface and shape into rolls and put these onto a greased baking sheet with spaces between, cover them with a warm dry cloth and allow them a further half hour in a warm place before brushing with warm milk to glaze them and baking in an oven pre-heated to 220°C. (425°F.) Gas Mark 7 for 15 to 20 minutes.

Galway, The Spanish Arch and The Claddagh Swing Bridge, C. 1865

THE PADDLE-STEAMER TUG-BOAT THAT BROUGHT OUR TRAVELLERS here was called the *Citie of the Tribes,* because Galway was called the 'Citie of the Tribes' by Oliver Cromwell as a gibe. The 'tribes' of Cromwell's sneer were some fourteen Anglo-Norman and English families that had founded the city under the leadership of Richard de Burgo following his being granted the Province of Connaught in 1226. De Burgo, aware of the economic and strategic importance of the site at the mouth of the Galway River, flowing out of Lough Corrib, built a strongly fortified castle and later a town on land which had previously been in the possession of the O'Flaherties and other Irish families.

In the course of time, the de Burgos, whose name became changed to de Burca, Burke (and also Bourke) had gone over to the Irish cause and been expelled from the city, leaving the fourteen Anglo-Norman and English families, by now rich merchants through trading by sea with Portugal, Spain and other countries, who formed the governing oligarchy. These families remained fanatically loyal to the English Crown and staunch adherents of Catholicism, forming a miniature English pale in the environs of their city. The dissolution of the monasteries and the rise of Protestantism in England brought about a weakening of that allegiance and this finally culminated in the siege of Galway by Cromwell and its surrender in 1652 and his disparaging epithet which the Galweigans have proudly borne ever since, regarding it a title of honour.

The open space beyond the bridge in the photograph is the old fish-market, with Galway Hooker fishing boats alongside the quay. At the south end of the fish-market is a fragment of the town walls pierced by a double arch, one archway of which is closed off. This, at the time of the photograph and for years afterwards was known in Gaelic as 'An Póirse Caoch', 'The Blind Arch' but today the arches are known, for no good reason except that the city traded with Spain, as 'The Spanish Arch', which undoubtedly sounds more romantic. The swing-bridge in the foreground used to communicate with the western side of the river and the Claddagh, a large village of thatched fishermen's cottages, with many traditions of dress and custom all its own, which was still in existence when this view was taken. In the Claddagh, it was customary for women to wear a gold ring with two hands clasping a heart and these rings are still popular today outside the area of the Claddagh and have been extensively copied. To the left of the photograph, at the end of the fish-market, stands a horse and cart ready to take away fish, though these must be for local use, as for distribution further away outside cars were employed since they were much faster, which was important for delivering fish to the coutryside around.

Leaving Galway for Clifden on the Bianconi Mail-Car, C.1870

Galway, although a rail-head at the time, would have had no rail services that could have taken our travellers further on their journey across Connemara and into Mayo. They would have had to leave the city on the Bianconi Mail-Car that ran to Clifden. As one may see, seating space is very restricted when all the places have been sold and sometimes there was overbooking on the cars, as Thackeray tells us (op.cit.) though this account referred to a journey from Kenmare to Killarney, it must have been typical on many of the Bianconi routes. 'The Irish car seems accommodated for any number of persons: it appeared to be full when we left Glengarriff for a traveller from Bearhaven, and the five gentlemen from the yacht, took seats upon it with myself, and we fancied it was impossible that more than seven should travel by such a conveyance; but the driver showed the capabilities of his vehicle presently.' When the seven of them were departing from Kenmare: '. . . a couple clambered onto the roof (actually the top of the coffer containing the mails, for Bianconi cars did not have a roof) where they managed to locate themselves with wonderful ingenuity, perched upon hard wooden chests, or agreeably reposing upon the knotted ropes which held them together; one of the new passengers scrambled between the driver's legs, where he held on somehow, and the rest were pushed and squeezed astonishingly in the car.'

'Now the fact must be told, that five of the new passengers (I don't count a little boy besides) were women, and very pretty, gay, frolicsome, lively, kind-hearted, innocent women too; and for the rest of the journey there was no end of laughing and shouting, and singing, and hugging.'

Let us hope that our imagined group had as entertaining and pleasant a car load on their forty-nine mile journey which they would have been wise to break, for the night, at Sweeney's in Oughterard, but, somehow, I think Thackeray had the more lively companions.

This Bianconi Mail-Car between Galway and Clifden was the very last Bianconi service to continue running. It was still operating when the railway connection to Clifden opened in 1895, but within a matter of weeks it had ceased, bringing to an end a unique form of transportation that had lasted for 78 years, whereas the railway that replaced it closed in 1935 after just less than forty years operation, giving way to the bus and the car.

Clifden Castle, Clifden, County Galway, home of the D'Arcy family, C 1865

The little town and fishing port of Clifden in Connemara was founded around 1812 by John D'Arcy of Killtullagh, a grand-nephew of the French soldier, scientist, Member of the French Academy and Jacobite, Count Patrick D'Arcy who was born in Killtullagh, County Galway, in 1725.

In 1815 John D'Arcy built Clifden Castle as a family seat where he could devote himself more easily to encouraging the growth of his little community, which had to depend much on fishing, sheep farming and kelp burning, when the latter revived with the increasing demand for iodine, but decline had set in by the time our tourists passed through. The tourist attractions of the area had not yet been developed; they would come with the building of the railway and bring a change for the better. Near here, Marconi established his first powerful transatlantic Morse transmitter, which sent the signal for the arrest of Dr Crippen and here too the first non-stop transatlantic flight landed in 1919. Being only a couple of miles from the little fishing port the wonderful selection of North Atlantic fish and fresh seaweed would be readily available in perfect condition here.

Turbot Cooked in Seaweed

1 large bunch of freshly gathered seaweed, such as Fucus, well washed in fresh water
1 medium sized turbot, cleaned
150ml. white fish stock, warmed
juice of 1 lemon
1 sprig of thyme, de-stalked, chopped
2 sprigs of fennel, chopped

Put half the seaweed into a turbotiére or into a very large casserole big enough to take the fish, rub the turbot all over, inside and out with the lemon juice, salt and pepper, then lay the fish on top of the seaweed and pour over it the fish stock and scatter over it the chopped herbs. Lay the remaining half of the seaweed on the top, put on the lid and cook on the hob at a fairly high heat for about half an hour, or until, when tested with a fork, the fish is ready to come off the bone. Have ready a large hot serving dish, remove the upper layer of seaweed and gently transfer the fish to the dish, keeping it hot while the remaining juices are drained from the seaweed and served in a hot sauce-boat with the turbot. Only oysters have a more deliciously marine flavour!

A Sod Cabin, or 'Black House' near Letterfrack, County Mayo, C. 1865

On the way to Leenaun, our travellers are now passing through one of the most desolate and poorest parts of Ireland, here, as in parts of West Cork and Kerry, the devastation of the Great Famine and land clearances had decimated the population in the most stringent sense of the word and those still determined to cling to the land often had to do so under conditions which today one would see only in famine stricken parts of Asia and Africa. Moving onto as yet un-enclosed land, there they built themselves shelters from the driving rains and winds with the materials available on the spot. The character of these structures is so primitive that they could truly be said to be much inferior to the better Neolithic houses. A depression having the plan dimensions of the house was dug to a depth of three or four feet, the earth being piled up around the edges. The earth floor was stamped flat and levelled so that it sloped slightly to one corner where a drain was dug to lower ground and filled with stones. Around the outer edge of the excavation a wall of dried turf sods was constructed, its chinks and crannies stopped with clay. The gable ends were made higher than the rest. Two forked branches of trees were lopped off short above the fork and their lower ends pointed and driven into the ground against the inner side of each gable. A long straight tree trunk or thick branch was trimmed and its ends supported in the forks at either end of the house, lashed in place with ropes made of straw or hide, to form the main central ridge support of the roof. Smaller branches were lashed to the ridge support and secured to the top of the turf walls and over these, strips of grass were laid with the clay side on the inside. Over this a thatching of reeds was applied and bound down with rope. Often, as in this photograph, large stones were placed, here and there on top of the thatch to give weight and help to keep the roof from being blown away. A hole in the roof let out the smoke from a fire on a stone hearth in the centre of the single room and piles of dried bracken or straw next to the walls provided the beds. In very exposed situations, earth was heaped up around the walls, giving the house the appearance of a small natural hillock as some of the very old Icelandic farm buildings appeared on the outside, as at Bergthorsknoll, but the latter were substantially constructed with a core of dry-stone walling and had many rooms and properly built chimneys and doors. This cabin is without any door, though it might have a curtain. The middle-aged father has boots, but both his wife and son are bare-footed.

A solitary wayfarer, Leenaun, County Mayo, C. 1865

Thackeray passed over this very road in 1842 and encountered another lonely wayfarer.

'He had been in the Dragoons, but his mother had purchased his discharge: he was married and had lived comfortably in Cork, for some time, in the glass-blowing business. Trade failing at Cork, he had gone to Belfast to seek for work, there was no work at Belfast; and he was so far on his road home again: sick, without a penny in the world, a hundred and fifty miles to travel and a starving wife and children to receive him at his journey's end. He had been thrown off a caravan that day, and had almost broken his back in the fall. Here was a cheering story! I wonder were he is now: how far has the poor starving lonely man advanced over that weary desolate road, that in good health, and with a horse to carry me, I thought it a penalty to cross?'

Such sights were still frequently the experience of travellers in the 1860s and, indeed, until the turn of the century.

Dooagh, Achill Island, County Mayo, C.1866

ACHILL ISLAND, SEPARATED FROM THE MAINLAND AT THE TIME OF our supposed tour by Achill Sound, a narrow channel connected at both ends to the Atlantic, is now linked to the rest of County Mayo by a swing bridge. Conditions then were poor, but not as poor as the parts of Mayo we have left, for the sandy, machair lands on the more sheltered, southward looking bays were fertile, though most of the island was barren moorland. The sandy land, manured by seaweed, grew potatoes well and the 'lazy beds' for growing them can be seen at the right. Fishing provided the other part of the economy and enabled small communities like this one to continue. The sandy nature of the soil can be seen in the photograph. On the higher ground sheep were kept. In the extreme distance, a little to the left of centre on the hillside, is a house, Corrymore Lodge where the celebrated Captain Charles Boycott, the Earl of Erne's Agent, later resided after his ostracism had added a new word to the English language. As an addition to their meagre income, the men of Achill were accustomed to selling to tourists amethysts which they pried from the rocks of Achill Head.

Such stones are still occasionally to be found there, but venturing onto those cliffs is exceedingly dangerous and better left to those who know their way about. Parts of the island have great charm of a westerly, remote kind and the best time for weather is September., when captivating dawns and sunsets are to be enjoyed. There are now several hotels, the most prettily situated being the Amethyst, in the little village of Keel, at the western end of Tr·more, the Great Strand, which stretches around for over two miles to the Cliffs of Minaun.

The village of Achill is on the mainland of Clare just to the east of Achill Sound and through it our party will have to make their return from the most westerly point of their excursion in Mayo.

The Midland Great Western Railway did not reach Achill until May 13 1895 and the first train to leave there carried the corpses of sailors drowned in a wreck. A local prophetess predicted that the last train to run on the line would also do so, which was fulfilled in September 1937 when the line was closed. Our party of tourists would have been obliged to endure a long drive by outside car to reach Westport before nightfall, but the railway having reached there on January 21 1866, they could have got a rail connection next morning although they would have had to go back as far as Athlone to pick up their train for Sligo, they would have in this way avoided a drive by exposed outside car of nearly seventy miles and reached Sligo in comfort at least an hour earlier than they would otherwise have done.

A stop for a cup of tea, Ardara, County Donegal, C. 1870

Unless they had come for the fishing, Sligo would not have detained many of our group for long, because the man who so tremendously increased visitors, interest in the surrounding countryside was still only five years old. Only perhaps Hardy, the Lakeland Poets and Dylan Thomas can have exerted such a powerful spell as W.B. Yeats in drawing such numbers to the regions they wrote about. County Donegal would have been the objective and after passing a night in Sligo they would have been off the next day for Donegal Town. Apart from fly-fishing, the great attraction of County Donegal at this time was the famous Donegal Tweed industry whose heart was the little town of Ardara. The wet mountains of Ireland, which are mainly situated around the coastal areas have been associated with sheep farming for centuries, but whereas the eastern regions have been mainly concerned with raising sheep for meat, the extra wet mountains of Connemara and especially Donegal produce sheep that have very thick, waterproof fleeces which are ideal for the weaving of tweeds. The Scotsman's woollen cloak and the Irishman's similar garment were not made of pure wool for nothing. Treated in the right way this wonderful material can retain its hydrophobic quality and retain body heat in a damp climate like no other natural fabric, while at the same time allowing adequate ventilation in a way that no synthetic fabric has yet succeeded in doing. Equally important in the damp climate of these islands, wool does not upset the skin-potential patterns of the body and so helps to ward off muscular cramp. In Ardara our party would have seen the spun yarns from the mountain farms being washed and dyed and woven on hand-looms to give the resplendent tweeds of varying texture, pattern and colour that have been irresistible to visitors for almost two centuries.

It is most interesting to notice the cleanliness and prosperity of this village which contrasts so greatly with the more remote villages of Mayo. The new slate roofs, though deplored by the lovers of thatch, show how the increasing wealth of the area is being re-invested in it, while the thatched roof of the house in the foreground has that special way of binding on the thatch so necessary in these extreme north-westerly parts where the Atlantic gales develop their full force.

After an exhausting day strolling around the weaver's houses and the warehouses, seeing the vast variety of individual tweeds, one feels confident that in this prosperous village a really satisfying tea can be enjoyed before the little girl and her mother rejoin the others at their hotel.

This meal, generally called in the northern parts of Ireland 'High Tea' is really the vestigial survival of the eighteenth century five o'clock dinner and always includes a meat course in which several meats are frequently served, as well as scones and cakes and sometimes a pudding too.

Shipquay Gate and Shipquay Street, Derry, C.1865

LIKE GLASTONBURY TOR, THE WOODED HILL ON WHICH THE CITY was later to be built, was once an island. An island in the estuary of the River Foyle, covered in oaks, it was known as Doire Calgaich, Calgach's Oak Wood and was possibly a pagan sacred grove. Granted to St Columba by Aimire Prince of Ui Neill, the saint built a monastery there in 546. Repeatedly pillaged after the coming of the Norsemen, it yet survived into the twelfth century and even became the seat of the Columban Order when Iona and Kells had both been abandoned. It was once again ruined in the Elizabethan wars and finally destroyed in 1600, when an English force led by Sir John Dowcra, arriving by sea, occupied the site and demolished the remains of the monastery and church to build a fort, leaving only a round tower standing. Around this fort a small town grew up but this, in turn, was obliterated by Sir Cahir O'Dogherty in 1608, leaving only deserted ruins. In 1613 these ruins and a great part of the surrounding territory were granted by James I to the Irish Society of London, a body of merchant adventurers who rebuilt the town and planted it with Protestant families, the walls being completed in 1618. Only twenty-three years later it withstood a siege by the forces of the Catholic Confederacy and a mere nine years after that it was again besieged, this time by the Royalist forces in the English Civil War, for the citizens of Londonderry, as the city was now called, had sided with the Commonwealth. Through this siege too it did not yield, but its greatest trial was to come in only another twenty years. In 1688, the forces of James II, defeated by those of William of Orange, fought a rearguard action in Ireland, during the course of which the City of Londonderry was called upon to receive a garrison from James II's forces. Lundy, the Governor, vacillated, but while he did so, his mind was made up for him by thirteen apprentice boys who seized the keys and closed the gates just as James IIs' troops were about to enter. During the course of the siege the besiegers rounded up hundreds of Protestants from the surrounding countryside and herded them under the walls, to starve, as an inducement to the garrison to surrender. The besieged then erected a gallows on the walls threatening to hang their prisoners if the unarmed refugees were not allowed to enter, after which the unfortunates were allowed to do so. Many of the refugees, the inhabitants and the garrison died of starvation before the siege was lifted by the food ships eventually sailing past the obstructions in the Foyle and bringing the desperately needed food in through the gate seen in the photograph on July 20 1699; the siege finally ending on July 28.

A Cannon on the Walls of Londonderry, C. 1865

Although, in Irish terms of relatively recent date, the city has, even today, many well preserved houses of the eighteenth century, which give it an attractive atmosphere that would have been bound to appeal to our visitors, as would many of the characters associated with the city. The Restoration dramatist George Farquhar was born there in 1678, but one of the most colourful personalities associated with its history is certainly Frederick Augustus Hervey, Bishop of Derry and 4th Earl of Bristol. He was consecrated Protestant Bishop of Cloyne in 1767 at the time when his brother, then the 2nd. Earl, was Lord Lieutenant of Ireland. Translated to the See of Derry in 1768, he took an active part in organizing philanthropic works, spending very large sums of his inheritance on building roads and the improvement of agricultural methods. He believed in complete religious equality and was opposed to the tithes system of financing the Church. Later, he took an active part in the Irish Volunteer movement and so vigorous were his calls for national independence that his arrest was contemplated by the authorities. With a view to bringing the Catholic and Protestant clergy closer together he organized steeple-chases every Saturday in which clerics of both denominations were encouraged to, and did, participate. He built himself several handsome houses and re-edified Derry's Bishop's Gate in a most graceful manner. Always fond of travel, he furnished his houses with many antiquities brought from abroad and when, in 1779, he succeeded to the title, he became a more enthusiastic traveller than ever. It is he, and not the city, that is commemorated in the numberless hotels 'Bristol' scattered throughout Europe. In 1798, while on his travels in Italy, he was imprisoned by the French occupying forces in Milan for a year and a half and died at Albano in 1803. He was known for his excellent table and his generosity to friends. This reputation was still current when Thackeray passed through Ireland thirty-nine years later. In spite of his eccentricities he must have had an engaging charm for he was liked and admired by two such exceedingly different people as John Wesley and Jeremy Bentham, no small achievement!

Derry today has the vitality of a city where many divergent views and outlooks are found together, giving it an energetic intellectual life that invigorates those who are able to enjoy the various cultural strands that create its unique atmosphere.

A Drink for Tourists at the Giant's Causeway, County Antrim, C. 1870

Almost at the northernmost tip of County Antrim, lies one of the natural wonders of the world, a stretch of columnar basalt of remarkable extent, formed by a huge intrusive dyke which cooled very slowly at great depth and pressure to form columns of regular polyhedral section, mainly hexagonal, but with rarer examples of four, five, seven eight and nine sides, and in one single instance three only. The dyke stretches beneath the North Channel and is seen again in the Scottish island of Staffa, where it inspired Felix Mendelssohn to write his 'Fingal's Cave' Overture. So regular and man-made does it appear from certain angles that ships of the Spanish Armada, endeavouring to sail westward into the Atlantic, fired upon it thinking it to be Dunluce Castle and one of them, the *Gerona*, was lost there with only five survivors. It has been one of Ireland's earliest centres of tourism and over a century ago made an ideal venue, as did the Gap of Dunloe, for interesting the visitors in local handicrafts. Nor were their creature comforts forgotten, for members of our party as they trudged the miles of pathways meandering through the strange landscape, would have found plenty of local people, such as this elderly man, ready to offer them a restorative, for less than three miles away was to be found one of the best distilleries in Ireland. The Irish whiskey that Bushmills distillery produced then and that which it still does today is one of the most distinctive and delicious to be found on the island.

Ten miles further east from the Giant's Causeway is the little town of Balycastle, known for its Lammas Fair, held on the last Tuesday in August. At this fair is traditionally sold an unusual toffee called 'Yellowman'. In her book *Traditional Irish Food* Theodora FitzGibbon has this to say about it: 'Yellowman is a toffee which has been made by the same family in County Antrim for several hundred years. The famous maker was a Dick Murray in Lurgan.'

1 heaped tablespoon butter
1 teaspoon bicarbonate of soda
225g. brown sugar
2 tablespoons vinegar
450g. golden or corn syrup

Grease a 25cm. tin with the melted butter and put into it all the ingredients except the bicarbonate of soda. Bring to heat stirring well so that all in the pan is well mixed and melted, then boil, without stirring until it gets crisp and a sugar thermometer shows 140°C. (290°F.). Then add the bicarbonate of soda stirring well as the mixture foams up (remember this when selecting a tin). When thoroughly mixed pour out onto a greased slab or tin and, when cool enough to handle, pull the toffee until it is a pale yellow, place on another tin, flatten the surface and cut into squares or sticks.

Carrickfergus Castle, Carrickfergus, County Antrim, C. 1865

O N REACHING BELFAST LOUGH AND TURNING IN TOWARDS Belfast our travellers would come upon, at the little port of Carrickfergus, one of the best preserved Norman castles in Ireland. In early times, when the estuary of the Lagan was shallow and the river obstructed by a sand bar, Carrickfergus was the important deep-water port. The rock on which the castle stands is a basalt finger pointing out into the Lough and tradition says that off this rock the Dal Riada King Fergus, from whom the Scottish Royal line claimed descent, was drowned after he had established the Gaelic settlement in Scotland from which the country takes its name. The Norman Barons John de Courcy and Hugh de Lacy had begun building the castle here at some time between 1180 and 1205. De Lacy was beseiged in it by Prince John, later King, who captured the castle after only a nine days seige and it is said to have slept there. From then on its history has been that of a Royal garrison castle, commanding the entrance to the Lough. Edward Bruce captured it in 1316 after beseiging it for a year, the long seige being possible because under the keep is a well in the basalt rock thirty-seven feet deep which provides fresh water., but it was soon returned to its original role. In 1690, General Schomberg stormed and took it from the garrison holding it on behalf of James II and shortly afterwards, on June 14, King William III landed at the quay to continue his Irish campaign which ended at the Battle of the Boyne and a commemorative stone still marks the spot.

In 1760, in a surprise attack, a French naval force under Commandant Thurot, captured both the castle and the town, but were soon repulsed by superior forces. Only eighteen years later, on the Lough within sight of the castle, took place the first naval fight in European waters of an American ship, when Commander Paul Jones in the U.S. *Ranger* engaged and defeated H.M.S. *Drake* and there is also another American association for the forebears of President Andrew Jackson came from the town Carrickfergus.

For a time the castle was used as a prison and a number of the United Irishmen were held there, but later it came into use as an armoury and magazine, the lifting derrick seen above the curtain wall at the right was probably in use for this purpose, but from 1928 onwards it has been a National Monument and much has been done to refurbish the structure and its interiors making it very well worth a visit today.

High Street, Belfast, in the Early 1880s

High Street is one of the oldest streets in the city of Belfast, dating from the seventeenth century. Near to the spot from which this photograph was taken John de Courcy built a castle in 1177 to defend a nearby ford across the Lagan and its confluence of another small river, the Farset. In the warfare between the Irish and the Anglo-Normans the castle was repeatedly burnt down until only ruins remained. The lands being then in the hands of the O'Neills of Clandeboye. At the Plantation of Ulster, the O'Neills' land was forfeited and granted to Sir Arthur Chichester, a member of a Devonshire family, who took possession in 1603 and on the site of the castle built a fortified house, which was originally the centre of a small group of thatched cottages though this soon changed as the settlers that Chichester brought over from the West Country and Scotland extended the village into a small town. The settlers obtained a Royal Charter for the town from James I in 1613. A little after his appointment as First Lord Deputy of Ireland in 1632, Earl Stafford gave to Belfast an important customs concession which he had purchased from Carrickfergus and the economic importance of the town began to increase and the port to be developed. After the Massacre of St Bartholomew, the mass arrival of Huguenot weavers fleeing France, who settled in Belfast and the neighbouring towns, assured the rapid development of the fine linen industry for which the region is famous to this day, and the beginnings of Belfast's commercial importance was further augmented by the establishment of a fleet of merchantmen, but as late as 1757 there were still only two thousand houses in the town.

A prominent businessman, Robert Joy, founded *The Belfast News-letter* newspaper in 1737 and he and Thomas McCabe introduced cotton spinning in 1777, however it was the commencement of ship-building by the enterprise of a Scotsman, William Ritchie, in 1791, that began to produce the rapid expansion of Belfast into the second largest city in Ireland. As late as the beginning of the nineteenth century the little river Farset ran down the centre of High Street, but soon it was to be culverted and great changes were to take place.

The establishment of the great ship-building firm of Harland and Wolff, in 1859, brought a demand for heavy engineering service industries and transformed the whole economics of the area, leading to further rapid expansion. Belfast was raised to the dignity of a city by Queen Victoria in 1888. At the eastern end of High Street can be seen the Albert Memorial, an imposing clock tower 143 feet high with a sculpture of the Prince Consort facing us. It was built in 1870.

Armagh, County Armagh, C. 1870

Armagh, from the Gaelic, Ard Macha, height of Macha, a pagan Goddess whose name is also associated with the nearby seat of the Ulster Kings, Eamain Macha, was the seat of those Kings after the destruction of the latter. St Patrick founded a church here around 445, first at the foot of the hill, but later, being offered another site, at its top.

One of the most important monastic schools in Ireland formed around it and led to the growth of the town itself. Though frequently raided by the Vikings, the school flourished and drew students from Scotland, England and Europe, but was finally utterly destroyed by the Anglo-Normans. Its treasures are now dispersed. St Patrick's Bell and its shrine are in the National Museum, Dublin, while the famous Book of Armagh, containing a copy of the New Testament, the Confessions of St Patrick and two biographies of the Saint, was donated to the great library of Trinity College Dublin by Lord George Beresford when he was Protestant Archbishop of Armagh.

On their way southward towards Dublin, our travellers will have been enticed to stay their course to take tea at the 'Golden Teapot' whose sign is to be seen on the right at the street corner. Partly because of the strong Scottish influence in Northern Ireland, there is a very fine tradition of excellent baking and the hungry travellers during the course of their tea, would undoubtedly have been offered some such provender as the following:-

Ginger Cake

225g. white plain flour
100g. brown cane sugar
50g. black treacle
4 level teaspoons baking powder
2 heaped tablespoons of butter
1 level teaspoon of powdered ginger
Half teaspoon grated lemon rind
2 well beaten eggs
Half teaspoon ground cinnamon
Quarter teaspoon of freshly grated nutmeg
A pinch of salt
225ml. boiling water

Set the oven to pre-heat to 180°C. (350°F.) Gas Mark 4. Take two mixing bowls, cream the butter and sugar in one and in the other sift together the flour, the ground spices, the baking powder and the salt making sure that they are evenly combined. To the creamed butter and sugar gradually add alternative amounts of the beaten eggs and the treacle, beating well so that they become evenly incorporated, then add in the finely grated zest of lemon, fold in the well sifted dry ingredients and lastly, add the boiling water mixing vigorously. Pour the mixture into a greased 22cm shallow baking-tin and bake for around 45 minutes and test with a metal skewer before removing from the oven.

Merchants' Quay, Newry, County Down, C.1870

The port town of Newry takes its name from a yew tree, Gaelic An Iubhar, which St Patrick is said to have planted beside a church which he founded at the head of the inlet of the sea, which gave the place its former name of Ceann Tragha, the Head of the Strand. Later, around 1144, an Abbey was founded at the site, where the yew tree was said still to be surviving after some 700 years. Nine years later, Cistercian monks from Mellifont Abbey took over from the original community, but again, only nine years later still, according to the Annals of the Four Masters, this Abbey and the yew tree were burnt at the same time. The Abbey was rebuilt by the Cistercians, but of the wonderful yew, which gave Newry its name, we hear no more.

In 1552, Sir Nicholas Bagenal, Marshall of the English army in Ireland, being granted the Lordship of Newry and Mourne, seized the property and converted the Abbot's House into a residence for himself and some twenty-five years later, in Newry, on the site of a destroyed de Courcy castle, built the first Protestant church in Ireland, the Parish Church of St Patrick, which though destroyed together with most of the town by James II's army under the Duke of Alba and Berwick in 1689, was soon rebuilt, though the main original feature to survive Alba's depredations was the tower. Bagenal's arms are still to be seen on his tombstone in the porch. Dean Swift, who held a benefice in County Down in his earlier days, remarked, of Newry:

> 'High church, low steeple,
> Dirty streets, proud people.'

It is to Bagenal and his colonists that the rapid rise of Newry as a port of consequence is due. After its sack it quickly resumed its commercial life and recognizing the importance of maritime transport to its growth, opened, in 1741, the Newry Canal, connecting the port with Lough Neagh, the largest lake in Ireland, which served to keep the port active throughout the eighteenth and nineteenth centuries. But this stretch of water, which would have been seen by our travellers, is, today, a car park.

Newry can also claim another distinction in the realm of transportation, for it was a group of Newry entrepreneurs who established the first mail-coach service in Ireland in the year 1790. It ran between Dublin and Belfast.

John Mitchell, one of the leaders of the 'Young Ireland' revolutionary movement of 1848, whose *Jail Journal* is one of the best known memoirs of Irish Republicanism, was born in Newry, the son of the Presbyterian minister, and his body lies in the old burial ground of the first Presbyterian Church there.

A Cutler and his Apprentice outside the Court House, Dundalk, County Louth, C. 1870

From Newry, our travellers could once again avail of the through connection to Dublin by rail, but we will suppose that they broke their journey several times along the way, first at Dundalk.

Because of its proximity to the main pass through the mountains into Ulster, the Moyry Pass, Dundalk was regarded as a position of strategic importance as well as a useful port. It takes its name from the Irish Dún Dealgan, Delga's Fort, a prehistoric fort which crowns a nearby hilltop and is associated also with the name of Cúchulain, The Hound of Cullen, a Red Branch Knight and mythical hero of semi-divine descent who figures prominently in a cycle of Gaelic folk tales.

In Viking times it was the main naval base of the Norseman Turgesius, who maintained contact by sea with his many settlements in Ireland, re-supplying and reinforcing them by sea though they were isolated from him by land and demonstrating again the Vikings' genius for exploiting maritime communications.

The territory of Dundalk and its surrounding lands was granted by Prince John to the Anglo-Norman Bertram de Verdon, who built a castle there around which the town grew and was fortified as one of the northernmost outposts of the English Pale, the main English defensive area in Ireland which was surrounded by an earth ditch and rampart topped with a wooden palisade, hence the name. Its geographical position rendered the area's history a tumultuous one, from the Iron Age right up to the Williamite Wars. Edward Bruce, surrounded by the leaders of his Irish supporters, was crowned King of Ireland on the top of Knocknamelan, close by, after taking the town by storm in 1315. It was saved from the destruction of a siege when King James II retreated from it ahead of Schomberg's approach, to take up his fateful stand on the Boyne River. In 1724, the days of walled cities being at an end from a military point of view, the walls were demolished. A most mistaken action from an historical and cultural aspect. The strong and dignified Doric Court House, seen on the left, is an early nineteenth century work of the famous Cork architect Sir Richard Morrison. But the town has other and closer links with Scotland, for Robert Burns' sister, Agnes Galt, is buried here, her tombstone still extant in the churchyard of St Nicholas' Church. The poet himself is thought to have made a visit, where other members of the family settled. It is interesting to note the cutler's name. It is not impossible that he was one of them. Another famous name associated with Dundalk is that of the Arctic explorer, Sir Francis McClintock who was born here.

An 0-6-0 Locomotive of the Belfast and Dublin Junction Railway crossing the Boyne Bridge.C. 1873

THE LINKING BY RAIL OF THE TWO MOST ECONOMICALLY important Irish centres though the second railway link in Ireland to be commenced, work beginning in 1840, only six years after the Dublin to Kingstown Railway was opened, was not completed until the year 1855. There were a number of reasons for this but among the most important of them was the barrier imposed by that most divisive of Irish rivers, the Boyne. Flowing through a deep valley with steep sides; broad and carrying swiftly a great mass of water, it proved to be a physically and economically formidable obstacle. To bring about the conjunction of the Ulster Railway's line from Belfast to Portadown and the Dublin and Drogheda Railway's line between those cities, a new railway company was formed in 1845 called the Dublin and Belfast Junction Railway and to it fell the task of bridging the Boyne. The plan was an ambitious one, two arched viaducts were to convey the railway across the steeply descending valley sides to the north and south banks of the river, at which point, from two massive abutments a single box girder would carry the double tracks across the water. Work was begun in 1851 and when the viaducts were in position a temporary wooden scaffolding was used to assemble and install the box girder span. Before the work was complete, in 1853, a small number of special trains between Belfast and Dublin and vice-versa, run in connection with the Dublin International Exhibition, were allowed to cross the wooden scaffolding, their all-up weight restricted to 100 tons and their speed to 4 miles per hour. It must have been quite a thrilling experience! The bridge was completed in 1855 and our travellers could have crossed it with equanimity for it proved adequate for double track working until the increased weight of locomotives and rolling-stock required what had by then become the Great Northern Railway to replace the span with a stronger box-girder, completed in 1932, and resort to single line working on the bridge. The author recalls passing many times across the old span as a child, but preferred the replacement as the more open lattice gave better views of the Boyne.

The photograph shows one of the Belfast and Dublin Junction Railway's new 0-6-0 locomotives, built in 1872, crossing the bridge, light, in 1873. The cab is not covered but the spectacle-plate is surmounted by a curved flange designed to give some deflection to the weather! The high steam-dome and tall, graceful chimney are noteworthy. The company owned two of these locomotives which they passed on to the Great Northern and which were not taken out of service until 1934 and 1937 respectively.

Gormanston Castle, Gormanston, County Meath. C. 1870

NEARLY A THIRD OF THE WAY BETWEEN DROGHEDA AND DUBLIN lies Gormanston Castle, at the time when this photograph was taken the principal seat of an ancient Anglo-Irish family of the name of Preston, who had held high Office of State since the time of King Edward III. Sir Robert Preston, Lord of Preston in Lancashire, was knighted in the field by the Duke of Clarence and shortly after this purchased the estate of Gormanston in the counties of Dublin and Meath from Almeric de St Amande. Viscounts Gormanston since 1478, the family have played a prominent role in Irish history in support of the English interest, but remained in the Catholic faith after the Reformation. The family crest is a fox, passant, proper and the dexter supporter of their arms is another, which may perhaps be the origin of a curious tradition which, until the early years of this century, was associated with this family. It has been maintained that when the head of the family is about to die, the foxes of the locality gather in numbers in the vicinity of the castle. Seymour and Neligan, in their book *True Irish Ghost Stories,* assert that when the 13th Viscount lay dying at the castle in 1876, only a few years after this photograph was taken, a large gathering of foxes was seen on the lawn surrounding the building and that, in 1907, when the 14th. Viscount's body was lying in the chapel, the Agent, being come there to pay his last respects, heard a scraping and snuffling sound at the door, opened it and saw a ring of foxes sitting outside. The 15th Viscount was killed in the First World War and the 16th in the second, but in each case no account remains of the appearance of any foxes. The castle is now a centre for Economic Studies. About ten miles south of Gormanston is a wide shallow estuary where wild duck are plentiful.

Fia-Lacha le Pórthfiona - *Wild Duck with Port.*

2 well hung wild duck, plucked, cleaned
juice of a lemon
4 tablespoons butter
salt and freshly milled black pepper
300ml. port, warmed

Rub the birds with the butter and roast in an oven pre-heated to 200°C. (400°F.) Gas Mark 6 for 20 to 30 minutes according to the size of the birds, season the port to taste with the salt and pepper and add the lemon juice to it, warm it well but do not allow it to boil, pour over the birds in the oven and baste at least once in the remaining 10 minutes of cooking. Remove the birds to a hot serving dish and keep hot while the roasting tin juices are reduced on the top of the stove, then pour them over the birds and serve at once.

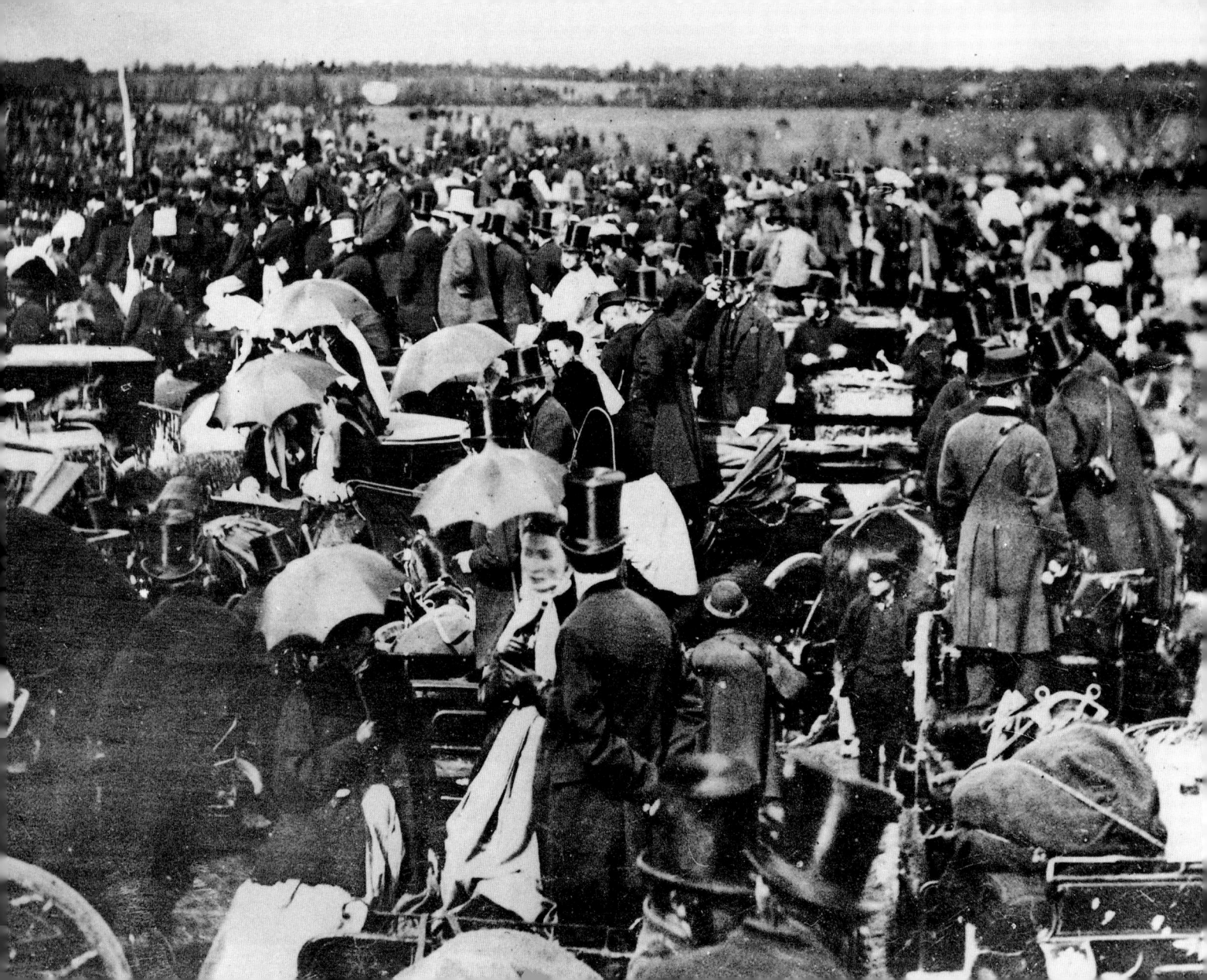

Punchestown Races, Punchestown, County Kildare, C. 1870

BEFORE QUITTING THE IRISH SCENE, OUR TRAVELLERS SHOULD experience an Irish Race Meeting such as this one at Punchestown, near Dublin. From an early hour, vehicles of all kinds, brakes, drags, Broughams, Berlines, inside and outside cars and traps, together with crowds of pedestrians begin to occupy the fields around the course and refreshment tents, roulette wheels and thimble-riggers' booths appear like an over-night crop of mushrooms. In the middle of the nineteenth century ladies were not seen in the refreshment tents or in the country public-houses in the vicinity. Their wants were catered for from substantial picnic baskets. Here is an example of a dish such as would have figured on such an occasion.

Chicken, Ham and Leek Pie

1 chicken of around 2kg., boiled and boned
200g. short-crust pastry
5 thick slices of ham
5 medium leeks cleaned and coarsely chopped
3 finely sliced shallots
salt and freshly ground black pepper
A little freshly grated nutmeg to taste
350ml. of jellied chicken stock
150ml. double cream
30g. dried tarragon
50ml. tarragon vinegar

The chicken should be boiled the day before in lightly salted water just to cover, to which the dried tarragon and tarragon vinegar have been added, until the meat is just ready to come off the bone. It is then boned and the meat reserved in a bowl in the refrigerator with a little of the liquor to keep it moist. The bones (without the skin) are returned to the stock and boiled briskly until the quantity of stock is reduced by half, when it should be strained to remove the bones and kept in the refrigerator over-night. Next day, de-fat the jellied stock, make the pastry, and, in a deep, 1.5L. pie-dish, set down layers of chicken, leeks, ham and the finely chopped shallots. Season the stock to taste adding the freshly grated nutmeg, pour over as much stock as is needed to cover. Place a china pie-centre in the dish. Roll out the pastry to fit the top of the dish, which should be dampened with stock along its edge. Place the pastry over and lightly press down its edges so that they adhere to the dish and cut a small nick in the pastry at its centre to allow ventilation, then brush the surface lightly with milk.

Bake on the centre shelf of an oven pre-heated to 180°C. (350°F.) Gas Mark 6 for 30 - 35 minutes, but cover with kitchen foil if it seems to be getting too deep a brown towards the end. Heat the cream, but do not boil it and when the pie is done remove it from the oven and carefully pour the heated cream into the interior through the central nick. Place over-night in a cool larder but not in a refrigerator and transport it to the picnic site in a cool-bag with its pastry protected from damage.

Leaving Kingstown (now Dunlaoghaire) C. 1885

Passengers who took their departure for Holyhead in the mid 1880s would have noticed a difference in the appearance of the City of Dublin Steam-Packet Company's vessels for they had just been re-boilered and now showed only a pair of funnels each. These remarkable ships remained in service until 1896, when they were replaced by new vessels powered by triple-expansion steam-engines driving twin-screws. Our party would have caught the train leaving Westland Row Station in Dublin at 6.40 a.m. and departed on shipboard at 7.00 a.m., with a calm sea, having time for a leisurely breakfast and a stroll around the decks before their arrival at Holyhead. How would their impressions of Ireland differ from those with which they might return today? They would certainly have been saddened by the extensive poverty in the slums of the cities as well as in the more remote rural parts. On the other hand they would not have been subjected to the hideous spectacle of rusting wrecked and burnt out cars and other industrial detritus which the present day traveller comes upon in unlikely places. But again, the mid-nineteenth century visitors would, unless they were scholars of the subject, have been virtually cut off from the vivid, living folk music and song, so readily available to visitors today. Such music would only have been accessible to them through Stephenson's bowdlerised arrangements for piano for accompanying Tom Moore's lyrics; popular in their day but sadly inadequate as an expression of Irish traditional music. Here the modern traveller gains enormously. The loveliness of the countryside and the captivating remoteness of the west would have been common memories to travellers in both eras. How good it is to travel. How good to communicate directly, rather than through intervening technological media, with other living personalities and to exchange with them impressions and thoughts about the world in which we live. Only by being on the spot can we be sure of finding out what things are really like. Today there is so much disinformation about everywhere, we need to travel to keep in touch with the real world, for we are surrounded by so many false communicators who are set on endeavouring to wrap us in illusion. Creative work is better fun than sport and actuality more strange than any fiction.

Arriving at Holyhead to catch the 'Irish Mail', C.1885

11.15 A.M., HOLYHEAD AFTER A FAIR CROSSING, SMOKE DRIFTING away on a mild south-west breeze and at the station platform, the 'Irish Mail'. Just comfortable time to disembark (there is no customs examination), have a telegram sent instructing a basket of lunch to be put aboard at Crewe and take our seats in the train. It leaves at 11.40 a.m. Those going north will leave us along the way and we shall arrive at Euston at 6.25 in the early evening.